With Liberty and Justice

Lynn Buzzard

While this book is designed for the reader's personal enjoyment and profit, it is also intended for group study. A Leader's Guide with Victor Multiuse Transparency Masters is available from your local bookstore or from the publisher.

VICTOR BOOKS a division of SP Publications, Inc.
WHEATON. ILLINOIS 60187

Offices also in
Whitby, Ontario, Canada
Amersham-on-the-Hill, Bucks, England

Unless otherwise noted, Scripture quotations are from the *King James Version*. Other quotations are from the *New American Standard Bible* (NASB), © 1960, 1962, 1968, 1971, 1972, 1973 by the Lockman Foundation, La Habra, California; the *Revised Standard Version* (RSV), © 1952 by the Division of Christian Education of the National Council of the Churches of Christ in the United States. Used by permission.

Recommended Dewey Decimal Classification: 261.7
Suggested Subject Headings: CHRISTIAN ETHICS; LAW

Library of Congress Catalog Card Number: 83-51315
ISBN: 0-88207-613-2

VICTOR BOOKS
A division of SP Publications, Inc.
        Wheaton, Illinois 60187

Contents

Author's Note

In these days of consumer fraud suits and disclosure requirements, we believe it only appropriate to warn you and to make a few disclaimers.

First, this is NOT an answer book. If you're wondering whether you have been cheated out of a fair share of Aunt Sallie's will, or how to be sure your assets will go to evangelism should you suddenly disappear in the Second Coming, this book will surely disappoint you.

It is not an answer book for two reasons. Sometimes there are no answers; sometimes we don't know what the answers are. But mainly, this book is about questions, trends, major issues, and Christian thoughts about law.

Even where we hold some strong opinions, we've softened them a little. We are sure, however, that some of you may spot a few biases. Here and there, you'll wonder if something isn't a wee bit too "liberal" or too "narrow" (or even too "stupid" or too "ridiculous").

Second, this is not a battle manual. While we believe there is indeed a spiritual warfare going on, and some of the skirmishes are in the areas we shall discuss, this book is not intended to either psyche you up for battling "them," or offer clever devices to use "the law" to get them.

The following chapters should help you identify some major problems, help you look at them as a believer, keep you on track, and challenge a few of your well-nourished illusions. This material focuses on the Christian perspective—our faith, our resources, our calling, and how our spirituality touches vital areas of law today.

1

Law Is
Too Important
to Be Left to Lawyers

You've heard that death and taxes are two things you can't avoid. There's another that's just as certain—law. If all the codes, statutes, administrative regulations, and ordinances are not enough, consider that there are 600,000 lawyers in the United States, and each summer about 40,000 new graduates are added to that number. All of these eager advocates are prepared to write laws, enforce laws, implement laws, hold you accountable to the law, and otherwise expand the application and uses of the law. Americans will spend $13 billion in legal fees this year—and that includes only private civil litigation, not the costs of courts, administrative agencies, and law enforcement.

Almost every arena of human activity is being invaded by statutes, regulations, and bureaucracies committed to the regulation of our lives. We see it in government regulation of economic life, in taxation, securities regulation, public housing, environmental law, and employer/employee relations. We are witnessing the "legalization" of human relationships.

Do Many Laws Make a Lawful Society?
One might expect from the increased number of laws and lawyers that ours might be a law-abiding society. But, alas, there are indications that quite the opposite may be the case. It has been

5

said that the lawfulness of a society is *inversely* proportional to the number of its laws. While a certain expansion of law may reflect increased moral sensitivities and a desire for justice, it is much more likely that laws expand precisely when there is a collapse of a more basic moral commitment. When a nation's ethical life ebbs, when a culture's moral resources are drained and people no longer do instinctively what they ought, it is then that legislatures gather to invoke the law.

The enormous expansion of law in American society may say a good deal more about our lawlessness than our love of law. Or maybe we love laws and rules to escape our larger moral bankruptcy. Food and drug laws, antitrust legislation, corrupt practices laws barring bribery by corporations in international trade, voter registration acts, securities fraud regulations: none of these laws emerged to reflect the functioning moral commitments with one another. Rather, these laws were a result of the failure of a moral ethic to govern our conduct. Such a recognition shows the inadequacy of law to provide the moral root for a society. Alexander Solzhenitsyn attacked the West's preoccupation with law, declaring:

> I have spent all my life under a Communist regime and I will tell you that a society without an objective legal scale is a terrible one indeed. But a society with no other scale but a legal one, is quite unworthy of man either. A society which is based on the letter of the law and never reaches any higher, is taking very scarce advantage of the high level of human possibilities. The letter of the law is too cold. Whenever the tissue is woven of legalistic relations, there is an atmosphere of moral mediocrity, paralyzing man's noblest impulses.

Woe to You Lawyers

The problem today with law is not merely that it is expansive and inadequate as a moral foundation. Rather, law itself is in deep crisis. Noted Harvard law professor Harold Berman has written extensively about the crisis in Western law. He declares there is a "massive loss of confidence in the law," that goes to the very integrity of Western civilization. This loss of confidence, he suggests, creates a widespread public distrust of the institution of the law and the profession of law.

Of course, law and lawyers have always been the subject of parody and ridicule. Some polls have suggested that lawyers rank with used car salesmen for trustworthiness in the public mind.

Some of the indictment of law is directed toward lawyers themselves and is reminiscent of Jesus' indictment in Luke 11:46-47, 52:

> Woe to you lawyers as well! For you weigh men down with burdens hard to bear, while you yourselves will not even touch the burdens with one of your fingers. Woe to you! For you build the tombs of the prophets, and it was your fathers who killed them.... Woe to you lawyers! For you have taken away the key of knowledge; you did not enter in yourselves, and those who were entering in you hindered (NASB).

Karl Llewelyn, a noted legal scholar, observed in 1933 that "the men of law are a monopoly," and critics as diverse as Ralph Nader and Chief Justice Warren Burger have complained that 90 percent of the lawyers serve 10 percent of the people. Nader referred to it as "a retainer stigmatism." As long ago as 1905, Teddy Roosevelt complained of the misuse of legal power on behalf of privilege, asserting: "Many of the most influential and most highly remunerated members of the bar ... may get this special task to work out bold and ingenious schemes by which their very wealthy clients ... can evade the laws." And famed jurist, Louis Brandeis, in the same year addressed Harvard undergraduates, noting: "Instead of holding a position of independence between the wealthy and the people, prepared to curb the excesses of either, able lawyers have, to a great extent, allowed themselves to become adjuncts of the great corporations and have neglected their obligation to use their powers for the protection of the people."

Today's complaints about law really go deeper than just the usual rhetoric about lawyers. The systems and institutions of law itself are charged with tragically failing us. Indeed, the charges against the system remind us of a prophetic indictment: encoding of wealth and privilege, unjust distribution of legal services, total failure of the criminal justice system, prejudice against the poor, fostering litigation and conflict, incompetence and lack of self-policing. In her book, *The Death of the Law,* Philadelphia Judge Lois Forer notes that law was once an honored, perhaps even worshiped, institution. Alexis de Tocqueville had suggested that lawyers were the "new aristocracy" of the new nation. But now, Forer declares, law has become an "obsolete faith" and the judiciary a "dying priesthood." We are a "nation of scofflaws," no longer obeying the law or willing to do obeisance before the robe of this legal aristocracy.

Surely law lost something of its aura and authority when Bob Woodward and Scott Armstrong wrote *The Brethren* (Simon & Schuster). They quote Chief Justice Burger as declaring: "We are the Supreme Court and we can do anything we want." *Newsweek* declared that *The Brethren* "delivered to the public with unprecedented detail and force" the reality that "judges are only human, and that their decisions often reflect personal politics, class, or viscera as much as a neutral reading of the law."

The Law Is King?

Far more serious is the breakdown of law itself as an institution in Western society. Law has played a very special part in the formation of Western democracies. It is a part of our American political mythology. We have prided ourselves that we are not a nation of men, but of law. We have spoken of law with a capital "L." We have praised legal institutions and language, spoken proudly of "rights," "constitutions," equal protection, and due process. These have been symbolized and eulogized in our schoolrooms, courts, and government centers. We proudly declare ourselves a nation of law. The "rule of law" is our noble achievement.

But it is no longer certain that our commitment to the rule of law is viable anymore. Harold Berman suggests that the Western legal tradition is in deep trouble:

> The Western legal tradition, like Western civilization as a whole, is undergoing in the twentieth century a crisis greater than it has ever known before. What is this crisis? It is clearly not that we do not have legal institutions or laws. It is something more basic. Law has lost its authority, its roots.

This crisis in law emerges from the collapse of our central beliefs and the *moral commitments* of Western civilization. In *Law and Revolution,* Berman notes:

> The legal systems of all the nations that are heirs to the Western legal tradition have been rooted in certain beliefs or postulates; that is, the legal systems themselves have presumed the validity of those beliefs. Today, those beliefs or postulates—such as the structural integrity of law, its ongoingness, its religious root, its transcendent qualities—are rapidly disappearing, not only from the minds of philosophers, not only from the minds of lawmakers, judges, lawyers, law teachers, and other members of the legal profession, but from the consciousness of the vast majority of citizens, the people as a whole; and more than that, they are disappearing from the law itself. The law is becoming more fragmented, more subjective, geared more to expediency and less to morality, concerned more with immediate consequences and less with consistency or continuity. Thus the historical soil of the Western legal tradition is being washed away in the twentieth century, and the tradition itself is threatened with collapse.

Law is helpless unless it is rooted in a fundamental moral and philosophic commitment. If the law is merely the word and opinion of the legislator, if it only expresses a momentary majority in some elective body, if it is functionally equivalent to the exercise of the power which comes from the barrel of a gun or the threat of prison, then law no longer really is LAW—it is merely an expression of power. We are really back to a nation of *men,* not law. The notion of *law* historically meant more than a statute. It meant something about "rights" and justice. Now law is divorced from truth—cut off from its source. It commands no respect, it bids no obedience. It is merely a threat. If law is not believed in, if it has no relationship to fundamental truth, justice, and morality, it will not work.

Such philosophic critiques of law, while they may go to the root problems in Western civilization, rarely are the frustrations perceived by individuals. More likely, our common frustrations are the result of such problems as the enormous costs of legal process, a sense that law is a "game" with its own unique and mystifying rules, prepared in such a way as to keep control of the game by the experts/lawyers. The average person feels confused, help-less, and angry when confronted with legal process. But these are symptoms. The more fundamental threat is much more profound.

The Christian Rediscovery of Law

In much of evangelical Christianity, there exists a deep suspicion about law. How can a Christian ethically engage in the adversary system, represent guilty clients, help people get divorces, argue in court for one side regardless of the truth, and participate in the murky world of politics? The sense that "lawyering" is dirty business is deeply ingrained in the Christian community. There's something just not right about a man who'll say whatever you want him to if you pay him enough.

But recently there has been a dramatic shift. A now successful lawyer who graduated from Wheaton College in the early 1950s, observed that during that period there was very little interest among Wheaton students in law. Back then, he knew no Christian lawyer personally, and to his knowledge, he was the only one in his class who had an interest in law. Today, scores of students at Christian schools look forward to becoming lawyers. Christian law schools have emerged in recent years, committed to the integration of Christian faith with the practice of law. LAW is "in"!

The Christian Legal Society is a rapidly growing professional organization with nearly 4,000 members. It is committed to the integration of Christian faith and practice of law, to calling lawyers to see the practice of law as an opportunity for ministry, for insuring liberty, for becoming legal peacemakers, for working for justice. Churches are even getting into the act. LaSalle Street Church in Chicago sponsors the Cabrini-Green Legal Aid Clinic. As a ministry of the church, this clinic provides legal representation of the needs of indigent persons in one of the country's largest housing projects. Christian magazines now regularly focus on legal issues, noting cases and important legislation. Religious political action groups urge their views of the law on the public.

Christian lawyers have been forced to come out of their closets. A new image of what it means to be a Christian lawyer is seen especially in young law students. In the past, it was sufficient for a Christian lawyer to be honest (and not misuse the trust funds), pious (go to church the proper number of times each week), help out the widowed, and aid the church with its property problems. But those images are no longer adequate. Present-day Christian law students observe that those old models of behavior really had nothing to do with law directly. Instead, Christian law students today need an understanding of being a Christian and a lawyer that goes directly to the task of "lawyering." If law is about power, about the institutions of a society and its values and structures, about justice, about human rights—about people with human problems—or about the making of statutes and enforcing of the criminal code, then surely one's Christian commitment must infuse all those processes. It is not enough merely to be a lawyer who is a Christian, but rather the demand is to be a Christian lawyer.

The interest in law is also seen in the myriad of groups which have developed largely out of frustration with law, and a sense that law and the courts have betrayed us, sold out our liberties, abused the authority of their offices, and led us into a sea of relativism and materialism. Countless groups have formed which have criticized the courts, especially the Supreme Court, have attacked the increasing interference with individual rights, and have complained that court decisions have coddled criminals.

Such an increased interest in law is encouraging. For too long Christians have avoided taking part in the legal process. We've been eager to complain of unjust laws, poor judges, and self-interested legislators, but we have not become involved in the judicial and legislative process. Churches have not encouraged gifted persons to seek careers in political life or in law. We have honored school teachers, missionaries, pastors, and doctors, but we've seen public life and law as a second-rate calling, and more often not as a calling at all. Who ever heard of a "legal missionary"?

No people who are committed to the biblical view of life can ignore the importance of law. But Christians must be aware of the limits of law in providing a sense of ultimate righteousness. Obedience to the law cannot "save" our souls or our nations. It cannot make us righteous. Nevertheless, law provides a critical structure for society. Law should save us from tyranny. It should teach us the truth and create an order of justice. Christians are by no means antinomian. We have too long left the law to someone else.

Some Questions about Our Legal Interests

This interest in law is appropriate, but not all of the ways in which the Christian community has responded are appropriate or reflect the real calling of Scripture. For many Christians, an interest in law has emerged merely because Christians are now the subject of law. We eagerly urge Christian lawyers to come to our defense, to protect the church from the civil authority, to excuse us from unemployment compensation tax, or the clergy from Social Security tax. At times, such "self-interest" may reflect genuine and urgent concerns for the dangers of entangling government authority with the affairs of the church. But as a fundamental basis for Christian involvement in law, it is surely inadequate. Our interest in law must involve more than protecting our turf or maintaining our independence. Our commitments to the character of law must be broader than excusal.

Popular books about law and especially about the courts paint a grim picture. Often these books infer that there is a conspiracy on the part of the legal process and perhaps the Supreme Court to strip from our society its moral foundations. Such rhetoric almost universally fails to take account of the complexity of law, the enormously difficult task which law has had in an increasing pluralistic society. Commentators, for example, who suggest that the Supreme Court is responsible for our society's hedonism, materialism, and the loss of religious commitments, know little about American history. Our materialism and secularism has far deeper roots in our educational system than in the law. Surely our legal system has been influenced by a positivistic spirit, but to attack law and the courts as evil conpirators is to be neither accurate nor constructive.

Much contemporary interest in law also fails to recognize the severe limits of law. In fact, the rush to law is ironic, given the trouble law is in and its weaknesses. If law has lost much of its moral roots, how can we expect it to lift up moral principles? Can law really rescue? Can we expect codes and statutes to catch up the hopes and dreams of a people?

Scripture recognizes the limits of law in touching the heart. When the consensus has been lost, when the church's evangelistic and educational mission has failed, can we then suddenly turn to the law and expect it to encode what we've failed to teach? Can we enact tougher criminal laws, create state machinery for the promotion of religious commitments, and really turn the tide? Surely not. A revival of character will not come from more laws, more police. It will come first to the heart. Then the heart being renewed, the law may reflect those new priorities.

What Should We Do?

What then is needed? First, of course, Christians must see law as a vital arena of discipleship. Law, religion, and morals are historically intertwined. There is a common philosophic, jurisprudential root in them which requires any society to think about values and norms upon which its law is to be built. Otherwise, law will become a word of partisan politics or the power from the barrel of a gun. Our involvement with law, based on our convictions about the nature of human life, is critically needed. Law is indeed too important to be left to lawyers.

Law today faces urgent issues. Law is confronted with decisions in the exploding biomedical revolution. Law must allocate power in an increasingly bureaucratic state with enormous instruments of information and power. Law must respond to human rights violations on a worldwide scale. Our society is inundated with drugs and crime at every level. Law must respond to these issues. In such a time, we dare not abandon the law to the technician and remain silent because we as Christians are untrained in law. We must not allow these issues to be resolved merely by those trained in drafting codes and litigating. There is too much at stake. We must have an active engagement with law—one that is vigorous, persistent, and principled.

It is urgent that our involvement with law focuses not simply on specific statutes or decisions, but on fundamental issues. Among the urgent questions are: What is the role of the state in the twentieth century, an age of technology, power, and regulation? What is the role of law? What is the relationship of law to moral values? How can we have a legal order with some moral base? Upon what common commitments should that moral base be founded? Ought not law to express not only a statement of reality, a sort of minimal ethical code, but in fact express our hopes and visions about what a culture and community ought to be? Shouldn't the law really be an invitation to a higher standard of duty than mere self-interest?

The task of our society, and of Christian engagement with our society today, is to avoid the temptation to harken back to an alleged golden age. In our contemporary criticism of law, we often look back to some past period in American history as expressing a nobler tradition to which we should return. Some look to 1776 and the Declaration of Independence, or to 1787 and the framing of the Constitution, or to the colonial charters and the deep religious commitments which were part of those founda-tions. If only the Pilgrims were here, or those no-nonsense Puri-tans—they'd straighten things out. The appeal is a simple one: Our nation was founded with a religious commitment built on the laws of nature and nature's God, and any other basis of public life is a betrayal of that commitment.

However, we must avoid the temptation to idealize a previous generation. No culture, no point in history has been signaled by God as normative. No time was without sin. We must read our history well and learn its lessons, but we must read even better the biblical mandates which come to us. Law in the colonies did not come directly from God. Law has always been a product of political and social process, and sin touched that law in 1787 as much as it touches the law now.

The framers of our constitution were brilliant persons who conceived an order of liberty which has become a wellspring of hope for virtually all the visions of the modern era. The ideals of human freedom, of limited government, may indeed be rooted in central biblical commitments, but the framers of our constitution did not necessarily catch all of the will of God about law. It is not our duty to return to 1787, but to determine what kind of legal order is appropriate for our day.

Such a recognition will help us avoid the idolatry of law and guard against our becoming nay sayers about modern developments. Positively, it will allow us to acknowledge substantial gains which have occurred in law. Not everything since 1787, nor even since 1960 has been bad. We have made enormous strides in such areas as civil rights, protections for the handicapped, and concern for the poor. Courts have often spoken out courageously for the "little" people.

Good men and women in legislature and the courts have sought, however imperfectly, to assure and expand liberties. Decisions of the Supreme Court such as *Brown vs. Board of Education,* barring discrimination in the schools, are not to be seen as low moments of a positivistic court, but high moments when a court sensed a higher law.

But there is a crisis today. As believers, we ought to heed the biblical insistence on justice. Theologian Markus Barth adequately expresses our vision: "The law remains one of the greatest and richest gifts of God. It is incomparable. It is a holy, righteous, and good thing."

That's quite an agenda for the church!

2

Justice, Law, and the Bible

A cartoon in the *New Yorker* pictured a client standing before his attorney, obviously pleading that his cause be defended and that justice be done. The attorney, in the words of the caption, then asks: "How much justice can you afford?"

Is justice for sale? Perhaps not, but it *does* seem expensive. Is law the same as justice?

Judge Learned Hand, upon leaving Justice Oliver Holmes at the Supreme Court, bid him to "do justice." Justice Holmes replied, "That's not my job; my job is to do the law."

If law isn't justice, if law is just a set of rules—sometimes fair, sometimes not—then isn't law in deep trouble? If law is merely playing by the rules, where do the rules come from?

Justice sometimes seems to be one of those words without meaning. Though it embodies the hopes and dreams of whole nations, it seems shorn of content. It often is little more than a code word for everyone's political agenda. Communists talk of "proletarian justice" and condemn "bourgeois justice." Iranians speak of "Islamic justice." We read of "social justice" and "economic justice." But are there really different kinds of justice? Is justice an empty concept to be filled with one's own ideas? Is justice merely the description we give to the legal system of those with the power, the votes, or the guns?

Jurisprudence: The Philosophy of Law

"Every law is a discovery and gift of God," declared the ancient Greek philosopher Demosthenes. His statement recognized the link between religion and law. From the earliest times, law and lawgivers have had a religious character. God was seen as the source of law. The law was rooted in God's will. It was often promulgated and enforced by religious authorities.

The moral content of law has always been tied to religious faith. In the past, the moral order formed the very basis for law. Law was not seen as merely the product of social or political process and power; it had to be rooted in truth and morality. As Samuel Stumpf observed, "Religious faith is the most powerful source of morality, and morality is the first version of the law."

The basic law of Anglo-American society, the common law, was infused with a moral base stemming from our Christian faith. Our legal institutions and norms were built upon a foundation of Christian thought. Even the specific rules which developed in the law of contracts, property, and criminal law often reflected specific biblical teachings. General principles of law such as truth-telling and equity were also deeply rooted in religious truths.

The whole debate about the nature and source of law and its relationship to religion, morals, and universal truths is the subject matter of *jurisprudence.* Jurisprudence asks questions too rarely addressed: Where does law come from? What is justice? Are there any standards by which law may be judged? Is a law still law even if it is evil?

These are not mere abstractions. They go to the heart of issues in our own day, and to the core of law itself. Law Professor David Funk writing in the *Capital University Law Review* observed that in law "the central problem is one of metaethics: how can we verify or otherwise justify the basic principles from which a moral code of justice is constructed."

Till recent times, there was little doubt in the minds of legal philosophers that there was indeed a standard for law. William Blackstone, the English law professor whose thought so deeply influenced American law, declared in his *Commentaries:*

The law of nature . . . dictated by God Himself . . . is binding in all countries at all times; no human laws are of any validity if contrary to this; and such of them as are valid derive their force and all their authority . . . from this original.

Blackstone echoed the thinking of Augustine and Aquinas: There is a higher law which God has built into the structure of the universe. Man's law must seek to conform to this higher standard. When it fails to do so, Augustine insisted, "It is not law." Law, to be worthy of the name, must not violate God's law.

In the past, there was a nearly universal consensus that law could not be arbitrary. Law was bound to a standard—that of truth and justice. And that standard was rooted in God's will as revealed through Scripture and, to some extent, through the natural order. This perspective is often referred to as a "natural law" jurisprudence. This view originated in ancient Greece, and many Christian scholars have warned about the tendency of "natural law" arguments to rely too heavily on reason and the natural order as opposed to revelation. For many Christians, however, a natural law rooted in God's fundamental standard was quite appropriate. Scripture and general revelation embody truths to which law was accountable.

In this sense, law was clearly answerable to religious commitments. Law, even when no longer administered by religious officials, and when totally secular in form, was nevertheless confined by eternal limits.

Such a perspective is not only historical. Many would argue it is *essential* for law. Harold Berman put it directly: "Law and religion stand or fall together." Lord Denning, recently retired Master of the Rolls in Great Britain, summed it up: "Without religion there can be no morality, and without morality there can be no law."

This linkage between religion and law was also prominent in early America. Thomas Jefferson, for all his willingness to separate church and state, still insisted that liberty was only secure when built on a "firm base," which is the conviction that laws are "the gift of God." The framers of the Declaration of Independence believed that certain fundamental rights were built into the order of nature by God. Their belief is apparent by their insistence on "inalienable rights" given by "nature and nature's God." During our nation's first hundred years and beyond, the courts expressed the conviction that American law was founded on Christian principles and the Bible. New York Chief Justice Kent declared: "We are a Christian people, and the morality of the country is deeply ingrafted upon Christianity." An early New York State Convention even declared that the Christian religion was the law of the land.

A Legal Revolution
Yet a radical shift has occurred. The concept that law ought to conform to a higher law, that law could be judged by some universal standards of right and wrong, has been almost totally rejected.

The attack on the concept of a fundamental and universal law began in earnest with utilitarians such as Jeremy Bentham (1748-1832), a contemporary and law student of Blackstone. He declared Blackstone's concept of a natural law as "nonsense built on stilts." Blackstone's view prevailed, but the victory was short-lived. By the middle of the 19th century, Bentham's view had carried the day.

Today, law is no longer seen as reflecting or being judged by any "higher law." Law is the command of the sovereign, the will of the legislator—that is all. Its rightness or morality is not relevant. It was Oliver Wendell Holmes who struck the note with a powerful image: "Law is not a brooding omnipresence in the sky." Holmes meant there is nothing "out there" by which to judge and select law. Law is merely the product of a social process.

Isolated from both morality and religion, law has become a political football. Law is the order of a sovereign, a power combined with a penalty for disobedience. "Do not—or else!" Law surely often includes that. But is that *all* law is—mere power and threat?

No one ever doubted that men made laws, and that social and political forces impinged powerfully on that process. Lawmakers knew that the "higher law" was often difficult to ascertain and convert into human statutes and rules. But till modern times, the law could be criticized by alleging it violated the higher law. It was subject to review based on its congruence with a standard. Now law is subject to no review.

This philosophy of law, whose sole interest is what *is* as opposed to what *ought* to be, is termed "positivistic" jurisprudence. Often the term "sociological" jurisprudence is used to reflect the emphasis on the social/political processes which make law. As a result of this man-oriented notion of law, the moral soil in which law is rooted has been washed away. Since law has become what one scholar called a "pragmatic human process" alone, how can we decide what law *ought* to be?

This rejection of ultimacy in law is simply a part of the relativism and humanistic emphasis of our whole culture. Reform scholar Hebden Taylor declared that such law is "man's declaration of independence from God." And with this independence, law is free to roam at will. Free, in fact, to wander to totalitarianism.

Positivists squirmed after the tragedies of German legal practice during the Hitler years. In Germany, where legal positivism had thrived, we saw a state doing everything "legally"—but something seemed tragically wrong. Suddenly, in the face of massive injustices, even positivists discovered that there were higher standards; these positivists helped prosecute Germany's political and military leaders for crimes that weren't even against the German law. As an outgrowth, we now have the Universal Declaration of Human Rights and similar proclamations concerning "crimes against humanity." These declarations all presume a higher law—a reality above our laws and politicians.

By rejecting the notion of a "higher law," today's law has no educative function. Law no longer calls people to something higher, for law merely reflects the state's authority through either raw power or majoritarian consensus. Law becomes technique. Law is whatever works or whatever the people want. With no moral reference, law has no morality except that of social opinion.

Rousseau's observation on the complexity of choosing just laws sums up both the difficulty of the task and the relevance of a

Christian perspective:

> In order to discover the rules of society best suited to nations, a superior intelligence . . . would be needed. This intelligence would have to be wholly unrelated to our nature, while knowing it through and through. . . . It would take gods to give men laws.

Our Relationship to God's Law

The biblical vision of law sharply contrasts with our own concepts. We think of the law as a necessary evil—a dry and lifeless set of rules to be enforced. Uncreative people called lawyers love to study these dusty volumes and add to them. It's for the weak, sinners, criminals.

Our vision of biblical law is often colored by a misreading of the New Testament. We have focused so exclusively on Paul's denunciation of the law as a means of salvation, and Jesus' condemnation of a legalism that distorts the law and turns it into an inhuman barrier to service and love, that we miss the profound biblical vision of the law.

For a biblical people, the law was a liberating and empowering gift of God. It came from God's very character as a moral being. It was as much an expression of His love as was His forgiveness.

From the beginning in the garden, God provided laws to give order, stability, and harmony to life. The creation of God's covenant people and their gathering in the Exodus was culminated in the giving of the Law—the Decalogue. This became the fundamental law of Israel. In one sense, the law created the nation and the community. It gave the people a culture, a moral vision, a character, a standard.

Beyond the Ten Commandments, God provided numerous ordinances and statutes to govern the civil, criminal, and religious life of the nation. Institutions of law, including courts, provisions for cities of refuge, and laws of evidence, were established to do justice.

Several aspects of biblical law are instructive. First it is a *moral* code. Its ethical character means it is not arbitrary, not merely a structure for maintaining authority and order. The laws provide a standard of righteousness and holiness.

Second, biblical law is a *community* code. It binds together the community, both to God and to one another. It establishes order, but it also requires that people live among one another in unity. Law is a social compact or covenant.

Third, the law is rooted in God's *personal command.* "I am the Lord" is the basis of the law. Thus His laws are often described as "testimonies" and "words." God adds the authority of His will to the law.

Fourth, the law is seen as *life-giving* and *redeeming.* Even the preamble to the Ten Commandments in Exodus 20:2 makes it clear that life is the consequence of obedience to the law. Obedience does not just make one "lawful" or "law abiding." Rather it is freeing, liberating, life-giving.

Fifth, Hebrew law is *practical.* Not much for theory, it is built around the exigencies of life. The system provides for a unified judicial system (Deut. 16:18; 17:8-13); it is to be fair to all persons, not showing favoritism (Ex. 23:3; Num. 25:15; Deut. 16:19); judgments are to be based on the facts (Deut. 25:1) without bribery (16:19) with a goal of justice (16:20). Punishment is to be strictly supervised (17:10-11).

But one may look not only to the character of the law, but to the attitude of the faithful child of God to this law. The Psalms give a striking view of this attitude to the law.

1. The law is a "delight" (1:2). It leads to joy, singing, and praise (105:45; 119:54, 62, 164); one "longs" for it (119:40); "pants" for it (119:131).

2. The law is worth meditating on "day and night" (1:2), so that it may be "stored" in one's heart as a preserve against sin (119:11).

3. Its value is "more than much fine gold" (19:10; 119:127).

4. It provides direction, counsel, and guidance (19:11; 119:24).

5. It is the real source of freedom and liberty (119:45).

6. It is a "shield," "hiding place" (119:114).

7. It gives peace (119:165), "restoring the soul" (19:7, NASB).

8. It cleanses with its grace (119:25-32).

Justice in Scripture

The Bible not only has a dynamic view of law, but justice is a powerful recurring theme. It is a central motif of biblical teaching and command. While the specific teachings about biblical law must be applied with great caution to our modern day since we do have a theocratic state, the teachings of the Scriptures about justice are fundamental to any society, and all people are subject to these principles.

Nothing so illustrates the centrality of justice in Scripture as the fact that the words for *justice* and *righteousness* are essentially the same. Justice is not a mere human, temporal interest in fairness. It is founded in righteousness. And righteousness is not mere ethereal interest in "spiritual" matters, but linked to justice. Justice exists when things are righteous, in right relationships.

The emphasis on righteousness is seen as well in the Old Testament prophets. Amos declared that God does not seek empty forms and rituals, but rather that "justice roll down like waters" (5:24, NASB). Micah insists: "What doth the Lord require of thee, but to do justly, and to love mercy, and to walk humbly with thy God?" (6:8)

The central biblical themes about the nature of justice are instructive.

1. Justice, like law, is rooted in God's character. God is a lover of justice. Justice is as much a character of God as are kindness and mercy (Ps. 99:4; 72:1-4).

2. Biblical justice is active, not passive. When Scripture calls for justice, it is not referring to abstract legal philosophy or great constitutional proclamations of rights and duties. Rather the command is to "do justly" (Micah 6:8). This is not an ivory tower examination of the philosophy of justice, but its specific implementation in the business and personal and political life of Israel. It is to be justice "at the gate"—the local court of the city where the daily disputes were settled. Justice is thus something very historical, relevant, immediate, visible. The people of God don't talk justice, they *do* it.

3. Justice is restorative and life-giving. Like law, the biblical teaching about justice is not a mere legal concept. Nor is it a mere weighing in the balances by a blind goddess of justice who assures impartiality. It is not merely punitive. Rather, God's justice is to save, to restore His people. Like His righteousness, justice is as much an invitation as a command. Justice is part of the work of God by which He reconciles man to man and man to God.

4. *Justice and the poor.* In Scripture, justice is intimately related to the widowed, poor, and oppressed. The vast majority of passages calling for justice are in the context of powerful indictments of ruling authorities who take advantage of the poor and helpless. Why this focus on the poor and widowed? Surely not because they are especially entitled to justice, nor because they are uniquely loved or worthy. There is not in Scripture the fascination, glorification, and romanticizing of the poor as in some contemporary literature and political thought. Sheer poverty is not a mark of righteousness. But there is a recognition that it is in regard to the poor and widowed and orphaned—the helpless of a society—that we may test the society's commitment to justice. The rich and powerful do not press any community's commitments to justice. They do not expose the fragility of our high-sounding talk. It is those without economic or political power, those not well placed to insist on their rights who put culture to the test. Here is the test of justice. They bear the brunt of injustice.

5. *Justice is hope and vision.* Often we think of law as simply a "conserving" force—providing a sort of minimum standard of conduct, keeping order, and protecting the status quo. Too often indeed, that is all law offers, but in Scripture the notion of justice and law is more than that. It is an expression of what God's people are to become as well as what they are not to become. Justice is a great prophetic vision to which Israel is called. The call to justice is a call beyond their present self-interests and narrowness. The justice due the stranger, pilgrim, and traveler presses Israel beyond her paranoia and provincialism. Thus the commitment to justice is to be inspirational. It pushes beyond the present. That is why justice is part of the vision of the new age when the kingdom comes. The new creation and the new covenant are filled with justice, whereas injustice is part of the present world which groans for redemption (Rom. 8).

Justice Today

If Christians are to follow the biblical mandate to "*do* justice," and if we believe that justice and law must reflect a fundamental moral and eternal perspective, we must begin to act in decisive ways on national and international issues of justice. Too often Christians have been unsympathetic, if not openly critical, of religious and secular groups that have been active in worldwide issues of justice.

Surely Christians, as others, may disagree vigorously about the character of many of the issues which confront us, which ones are urgent and even on which side truth rests. But for us to be silent in the face of massive injustices which wrack our world is to fail to hear the links between justice and righteousness and to fail to know a God who is a "lover of justice."

The Christian engagement must be at many levels. Raising awareness of issues, educational efforts, advocacy of government policies, direct involvement through non-governmental agencies— all these are legitimate avenues of response.

It is with hesitancy that we suggest any particular issues of justice. Many will believe we have surely omitted what they believe is of paramount importance, others may even disagree. But nevertheless we believe there are several issues on which there ought to be near universal agreement and involvement on the part of the Christian community.

Hunger. The tragic loss of life, the personal suffering, the wasted human resources are some of the effects of continued massive hunger in the world. The Christian community ought to be leading the efforts both to alleviate the immediate symptoms as well as to encourage appropriate economic, scientific, and political action which can touch this blot on our world. The interplay of economic, political, and cultural dimensions may exascerbate the problem, but are not excuses for inaction. Groups such as World Vision, Bread for the World, and others are seeking to provide leadership. Only as the church sees the enormous moral dimensions of this issue will there be the will and resources necessary to offer any hope at all. A world capable of placing men on the moon, packaging billions of dollars worth of video games, and feeding a vast population of pets can clearly do more.

Human Rights. A tragic consequence of American isolationism and the church's parochialism is the almost universal unawareness in the church of the violations of human rights which take place throughout the world. Rights we declare as inalienable and God-given are only dreams for much of the world which lives under totalitarian regimes of both the left and right.

Human rights violations in the Soviet Union are legendary. In recent years, Jewish and Christian groups have come under increased surveillance, harassment, and persecution. Jewish emigration has been cut to a trickle with "refuseniks" (Jews who have applied for, but have been denied permission to emigrate) suffering severe economic reprisals, including the retroactive revocation of college degrees. Christian leadership in Lithuania is under heavy assault. The World Psychiatric Association has expelled the Soviet branch for the continued use of psychiatry as a means of punishing dissidents who are confined to hospitals.

South African policies of apartheid, the continued tragedies in Southeast Asia especially Cambodia, and violation of human rights in the Middle East are outrages.

That these are difficult, apparently intractable problems for effective political and religious action is not a sufficient basis for silence. The problems extend beyond the Christian community, but at least we ought to sense our oneness with the suffering church throughout much of the world. Groups such as Keston College, U.S.A., and CREED are active in dealing with religious persecution. Amnesty International and government reports on compliance with the Helsinki Accords provide a broad spectrum of violations of human rights, including prison sentences without trials, massive torture, political imprisonments, religious discrimination.

Civil Rights. Since the abolitionist crusades of the mid-19th century, churches have taken the lead in almost every genuine effort at reform, such as abolition of slavery, child labor laws, prison reform. The record of the church at large in the more modern civil rights movement has been less impressive. Evangelicals stood largely on the sideline while their more liberal colleagues marched in Selma, gathered in Washington at the mall, and worked for voting rights, fair housing legislation, equal opportunity employment, and desegregation of schools.

Candor requires our admission that racial prejudice has been a characteristic of our society and touches many of us individually. Such attitudes have been evidenced as well in the treatment of American Indians and other minorities. Our society continues to pay a toll for its sin in this regard.

There is a legitimate debate about the best way to implement and express our commitments to equality before the law, and to attain the high goal of building national and local communities without regard to racial prejudice. But while debates will persist about affirmative action, busing, etc.—there can be little debate that under the Gospel we have a high duty toward one another that compels us and our churches to speak and act in ways which are appropriate to our oneness in Christ.

Some occasionally suggest that advocates of justice are too strident, too critical, too self-assured in their judgments about what is just. They complain that such an emphasis is a "social gospel."

Precisely the same charge was leveled against the prophets. Amos was told to go home and mind his own business. Jeremiah was accused of not being a patriot and shipped off in exile. Their meddling in the affairs of the state and economic life were no doubt criticized by those who could not believe that what was, fell short of God's will.

How can we as Bible-believing people doubt for a moment that the God who shatters our own self-centered lives and calls for a total reorientation of our way of life and thinking, should not call a nation to such radical renewal as well? There is no biblical base for believing that the way things are now is what God wants. To the contrary, we ought to expect that God's justice and His economic order and political order will be quite different from our human systems. To think, therefore, that our present system of justice is not to be challenged or disturbed by God's people would be to deny His lordship, sovereignty, and authority as Judge.

3

There Ought
to Be a Law

For which of the following would you favor a public law that
penalizes the prohibited conduct?
1. The use of contraceptives within a marriage
2. Impermissible forms of sexual relations between married persons
3. Fornication
4. Failure to attend church regularly
5. Homosexual acts between consenting adults
6. "R" rated movies
7. Discriminating against minorities in private employment
8. Polluting the environment with toxic wastes
9. Literature which contains language defaming to Jesus Christ

* * * * *

A study conducted by the Connecticut Mutual Life Insurance
Company concluded that "moral issues have vaulted to the fore-
front of political dialogue. . . . Something unusual is happening."

It really wasn't necessary for them to tell us. It is abundantly
and tragically apparent. Crime, divorce, and drug statistics put
the tragedies in charts and tables. The historic and nurturing
commitment of American society to the Judeo-Christian moral
perspective is under assault on almost every front: in law, in
philosophy, in media, and in education. Christians are either
blissfully ignorant (happily attending the church of their choice)
or appalled. We have already lost the capacity to be shocked!

Moral pluralism is in. What began as a seemingly innocuous and perhaps proper decriminalization of some private conduct; what appeared to be simply a less repressive and open perspective; what reflected more sensitivity to minority perspectives—has become a full-blown moral revolt. We are experiencing what Alvin Toffler called "value vertigo." Conduct once prohibited under penalty of law (such as homosexual conduct or raw hardcore pornography), has not only been decriminalized, but is increasingly protected. Now those who continue to insist such conduct is wrong are labeled the wrongdoers for "discriminating," or at least marked as morally backward and unenlightened.

The shedding of moral restraints is in keeping with the relativistic consensus of modern thought. "Ethics are autonomous and situational," insists the *Humanist Manifesto II*. Many, quite unfamiliar with such a declaration, and perhaps not even knowing the word *autonomous* put it more directly: "Do your own thing." Moral values are relative, and thus of course, there are no ultimate moral truths.

The law has been touched by the same spirit. The law is faced with increasing pleas to decriminalize supposed "victimless crimes"—drug use, prostitution, gambling. Homosexual caucuses pressure courts to give legal status to their claimed rights of marriage, adoption, and freedom from "discrimination." In San Francisco, a homosexual even sought to use a city ordinance barring discrimination in employment to gain a judgment against a church for dismissing him as their organist.

The signs of moral pluralism are all about us. Visit a 7-Eleven convenience store or chain book shop and note the magazine racks, or check the advocacy of what are euphemistically called "alternative lifestyles" on television.

Indeed, the media have played a major role in the assault on moral values. James Hitchcock, professor at St. Louis University, has noted the dramatic, and not accidental, shifts in the media since 1965. He writes:

Put simply, those who controlled the media realized that there was a substantial audience which had broken with traditional moral values and wanted entertainment that ventured into forbidden territory in hitherto forbidden ways. Not only were taboo subjects treated, they were treated iconoclastically; traditional moral values were ridiculed, assaulted and ground into dust. . . . The manipulators of the media also suspected, correctly as it turned out, that many people who professed traditional values would nonetheless accept the new iconoclasm simply as entertainment, without examining too closely the values behind it. The moral corruption which affected many good people in America was nowhere more ruthlessly revealed than here.

Enter the Law

In the face of this moral collapse, many Christians turn hopefully to the law. Can't the law restore our moral foundations?

But there are problems in relying on the law. Who decides what the moral values are, and which ones ought to be in the public laws? What about freedom? What about the will of the majority? Or of the minority? What is the purpose and limit of law in regard to moral conduct? Can morality be legislated?

Some principles which we believe in tend to argue for such a use of the law.

1. There is a moral law. Christians and others insist that there is intrinsic right and wrong. Morality is not a mere product of social and political power or the remnant of our fears of the unknown. The moral law is not frivolous; rather, it is fundamental to our character. We cannot ignore it with impunity. Our fulfillment, our happiness, and our wholeness are lost when we fail to live by the moral law.

God stands in judgment over both persons and nations in regard to the moral law. We risk our nation's life when we reject God's moral commands. "Righteousness exalts a nation: but sin is a reproach to any people" (Prov. 14:34).

2. Law is inescapably moral in character. Law is always and inevitably linked to morality. You can't legislate moral people, but you can mandate right conduct and punish immoral conduct. Norms, ethics, and moral convictions are the bases of both civil and criminal law. All law is "moral," either directly or indirectly.

Legislation regarding drug usage, child labor, age of consent, discrimination, theft, contracts—all are rooted in moral and ethical convictions.

In fact, we often say that a prohibited act is "wrong," and not merely that it is "illegal." But on what basis should the law judge some conduct illegal if it were not, at least indirectly, "wrong"?

Indeed, the irony in the rush to excise so-called "private" morality from the law, is that there is an enormous expansion of law today which is rooted in notions of moral and ethical values. The sensitivity regarding issues of discrimination, economic regulation, interest in international human rights never emerged merely out of majoritarian politics, but out of moral judgments. Such laws regularly invade my "turf," and proponents are not impressed with any plea I might make that they are imposing "their" morality on me.

The issue is not whether law can encode morality, but what morality shall it represent? What basic moral principles shall shape the law? And what components or aspects of that morality are appropriate for enforcement by the law?

3. *Liberty assumes structure.* The uncritical hailing of "liberty" and freedom as a basis for eliminating moral components in law is deceiving. Of course laws based on moral viewpoints would restrict "liberty." All laws do that. Laws barring me from disposing of my mother-in-law, driving down the left side of the road, or opening my own sewage disposal plant in my backyard, all restrict liberty. But only in a narrow sense. In a larger sense, law provides for liberty. Law creates a structure for channeling and ordering life that enhances actual liberty as opposed to the illusory liberty of disorder. Liberty and freedom are not increased as the number of laws are decreased. Freedom and liberty, both in the public and personal context, emerge when they are rooted in the discipline of values and norms. No society could have liberty without a political consensus. That would be anarchy.

It seems clear that there can be no such thing as a "totally" neutral state, uninhibited in its freedom. Notwithstanding, "pluralism" has its limits. Pluralism, properly understood, seems not only inevitable, but good. Christians need not fear the marketplace of ideas or the lack of government endorsement for sectarian purposes. Christians, after all, did quite well in the first century with nary a prayer breakfast. Pluralism will compel us to be more rigorous in our apologetics and evangelism. It will separate chaff from wheat. Religion will be less "popular." Minorities will likely find less endemic discrimination in employment and housing.

But unbridled pluralism is intolerable. Michael Farris, founder of the First Freedoms Foundation, has correctly observed that pluralism as to fundamental values is impossible. One cannot be "pluralistic" about racial prejudice, theft, the holocaust, and religious liberty. All values are not up for grabs on an individual basis.

4. *The state as moral educator.* Most Christians see a positive duty in government to sustain the good as well as to restrain evil. Such a perspective emerges not only in the Old Testament with its theocratic state, but in the teaching of Paul in Romans 13.

The classic view from ancient Greece till the 19th century was virtually unanimous in insisting that the state should nurture and encourage moral advancement. The state was not merely to keep the peace or conduct foreign affairs and maintain the road. It possessed a public duty.

Contrasting sharply with such a view, however, is one like that of John Stuart Mill who insisted that government ought to interfere as little as possible with one's individual liberty.

> The only purpose for which power can rightfully be exercised over any member of a civilized community against his will is to prevent harm to others. . . . His own good, either physical or moral, is not a sufficient warrant.

Mill's view has come to dominate our thinking today. It was restated by the famous Wolfenden Commission, appointed by Parliament to study the issue of the decriminalization of homosexual conduct:

> [The] function [of the criminal law], as we see it, is to preserve public order and decency, to protect the citizen from what is offensive or injurious, and to provide sufficient safeguards against exploitation or corruption of others, particularly those who are especially vulnerable because they are young, weak in body or mind, or inexperienced. . . . There must remain a realm of private

morality and immorality which is, in brief and crude terms, not the law's business.

At first this report did not seem all that controversial. Surely some things are not any business of the law. But what does "preserve public order and decency" mean?

It wasn't long till a historic debate was joined between Lord Devlin and H.L.A. Hart, an American law professor at Harvard. Devlin insisted that private vice was indeed a legitimate business of the law. A nation had a duty to protect itself from subversion, not only of a political nature, but morally as well. Morality is the cement of a society, and there is a duty to protect that culture from disintegration.

George Will in his *Statecraft as Soulcraft* (Simon & Schuster), while not specifically addressing the morality issue, seems to affirm a moral task for the state. Will insists "there is only one 'first' question of government, and it is 'How shall we live?' " Yet for two centuries, Will insists, there has been a "reckless neglect of the moral world." We have forgotten about a concern for the public good, and redefined it simply as "a lumpy stew of individuals and groups." He calls this the "Cuisinart theory of justice."

Will sees a tragically skewed emphasis by the state on enabling economic development, but not that of the "soul." He concludes, "It is time to come up from individualism. . . . And we need a public philosophy that can rectify the current imbalance between the political order's meticulous concern for material well-being and its fastidious withdrawal from concern for the inner lives and moral character of citizens."

Limits of the Law
Our commitment to an absolute moral law, binding on all persons and government, and a recognition that law is inevitable and necessarily moral in character, are NOT enough to solve our dilemmas. Certain aspects of Christian faith and our public lives significantly limit the use of law to enforce some kinds of morality.

1. The inherent limits of law. In our rush to defend our moral character with the law, we can too easily ignore the limits of such a Maginot Line approach. Law by its very character is simply unable to carry all the freight of the moral life. Lord Devlin, who was an advocate of the use of the law to protect fundamental morals, nevertheless insisted, "If the dead weight of sin were ever allowed to fall upon the law, it could not take the strain."

The law can never encompass the limits of morality. It cannot touch the key to moral life—the "heart," the intentions of humankind. The Scriptures make this point powerfully. The law cannot save; one may keep the letter, but lose the spirit; the law creates guilt, not redemption (2 Cor. 3:3-6; Rom. 7:6). The prophetic longing for the day when the law is written on the heart is an acknowledgment of the limits of laws written on parchments (see Jer. 31:33). In fact, one Christian commentator warned about law meddling with morals, lest it interfere with the work of the Spirit. The genuine moral life is one of choice, not of command.

The state has means other than law to nurture moral life. The law, because of its penal and intrusive character, may at times be an improper and unwise tool, but that does not mean the state may not counsel and encourage moral life. The state may use educational institutions, government benefit programs, tax preference policies, and its power of moral persuasion by leadership to counsel higher moral standards. While, for example, the law may not be an appropriate tool to deal with infidelity in marriage, that does not mean the state may not "teach" and model its commitment to family integrity. Christians have given far too little attention to the potential in this area for governmental support of moral principles, and government leadership has mistakenly thought that because many acts reflecting different values are *legal* that they are all equal *morally* and equally entitled to government benefits. We need a national and cultural leadership which speaks clearly and unequivocally on moral issues, even when law is inadequate.

2. *The law as a snoop and busybody.* The Wolfenden Report proclaimed that there are some things that are none of the law's business. Most of us would agree. When Connecticut barred the use of contraceptives (in effect enforcing a moral rule as perceived by the Catholic community), the United States Supreme

Court struck the statute down as unconstitutional. The Court did not evaluate the morality of the policy, but spoke about a fundamental right of "privacy," especially in the context of marriage and the family. While the Court acknowledged that the Constitution did not give such a privacy right in specific terms, it was a right so basic that it was woven within the fabric of the entire Constitution.

In much of the contemporary debate about moral laws, the real substance is NOT whether morality ought to be enforced by law, but what aspects of morality are really "public" (legitimate interests of the state) and what are "private" (areas where government ought to mind its own business). What acts are sufficiently private (both in their performance and their consequences) so that there is simply no legitimate public interest at stake? These are not easy determinations. Certain acts, thoroughly private and with no immediate and directly traceable public consequences, nevertheless have profound social consequences, e.g., gambling, pornography. Where should the line be drawn?

Advocates of decriminalizing so-called "victimless crimes" (such as pornography, gambling, homosexual conduct), claim these are "private" decisions of consenting adults, and thus no business of the law. What people willingly choose to do in the privacy of their homes, the Supreme Court has noted in some cases, is not the business of the law.

But it is quite inadequate simply to insist on non-interference with acts merely because they are done by consenting persons. Our laws are replete with examples of state interference where both parties are quite happy with what they are doing. A minor might consent to sexual abuse, a child to work in a factory, an immigrant to forego social security or minimum wages, a drug purchaser to buy, but the law will not be impressed with objections that it is being "paternalistic." So-called victimless crimes provide a whole society of harm in broken relationships, economic waste, and demoralized human spirits.

3. *Big Brother is watching.* Since our doctrine of sin encompasses the immorality of governments as well as of individuals, we should not view the government as a Father setting forth the

rules of our lives. While political columnist George Will's idea of "soulcraft" sounds immensely appealing to those who see too often a valueless national leadership, the history of the exercise of power by the state is that indeed "power corrupts." Countries which are engaged in "soulcraft" have clear visions of how their people ought to live; their governments use their law to create such norms. The clearest examples are the Soviet Union, China, Cuba, South Africa, Libya. These are not permissive states; they do not wallow in indecision.

4. A price of liberty. While liberty is not without order, neither can it thrive without permitting a significant degree of dissent—ornery, irascible malcontents who flaunt majoritarian views. There are always tensions between the interests of liberty and of order, tyranny and anarchy. From the beginning, our American system chose to err on the side of a certain degree of disorder as a necessary price of liberty.

But evangelical Christians have tended to be a little schizophrenic about the role of the state. Often we have advocated a very liberty-oriented view of the state in respect to economic and social regulation (opposing government interference with business, meddling in social engineering, etc.), but held to an aggressive policy in areas of enforcement of morals. Contemporary liberals express the same confusion, only in reverse—happily urging increased government restraint of what they see as improper business activity or social sin, but totally opposed to government involvement with traditional moral areas.

This commitment to a strong component of liberty, relates as well to the pluralism and diversity of our society. There is a sense of a social compact in a democracy to respect minority interests, and perhaps only to intrude where there is a compelling interest. Respect for minorities has not been, however, a Christian longsuit. We are often insensitive to those whose moral views are distinctly different from our own. Perhaps now that Christian perspectives are increasingly a minority viewpoint, we can recognize the high value of tolerance.

5. The Khomeni complex. Recent events in Iran and the Islamic revolution illustrate what happens when a government becomes a moral order and reflects the commitments of a religious faith. While efforts to restore moral principles in American life should not be tarnished by a simplistic comparison to events such as in Iran, Christian history has as well its less than admirable record at distinguishing central moral principles from the peculiarities of both the time and the leadership. John Calvin, with a conviction that God's law ought to be the law of the state, persuaded the Geneva city council to pass laws against playacting and watering down wine. But as Fuller Seminary Professor Lewis Smedes reflected, "His evangelical motives were sound. But even a Reformed CIA, strolling around at private birthday parties and wedding receptions, was hard for Calvinists to take."

Pragmatism

Let's suppose you've leaped these hurdles of policy and principle. There still remain some questions. Suppose, for example, one concluded that smoking was one of those central issues of morality that warranted the interference with individual liberties. There remain some tough questions. Without answering them, let's simply create a checklist of some pragmatic aspects which must be included in our decision about the legal enforcement of morals:

1. Is the prohibition enforceable?
2. Is the enforcement carried out in such a way as not to create inordinate invasions of privacy or to create a police state so that the cure is worse than the disease?
3. Could and would the enforcement be fair?
4. Is the contemplated punishment appropriate?
5. Is there a sufficient public consensus so that the law is respected?
6. Is the criminal law the best instrument for control of this behavior?
7. Will the criminalization of this conduct actually diminish its incidence?
8. Will enforcement of this prohibition unwisely divert limited law enforcement, judicial, and correctional resources of the government?

All these cautionary notes may create so many exceptions that indeed we might as well forget law as an ally. The observation of columnist Russell Kirk puts perhaps the whole issue into a proper perspective:

> I venture to suggest that the corpus of English and American laws . . . cannot endure forever unless it is animated by the spirit that moved in the beginning: that is, by religion, and specifically the Christian religion. Certain moral postulates of Christian teaching have been taken for granted, in the past, as the ground of justice. When courts of law ignore those postulates, we grope in judicial darkness.

4

The Battle for Religious Liberty

Answer the following statements true or false:

1. The Constitution declares that there shall be a wall   T   F
of separation between church and state.

2. The Supreme Court poses the most serious threat   T   F
to our religious liberty.

3. We have less religious liberty today than at any   T   F
time in our history.

4. We need a constitutional amendment to insure   T   F
religious liberties.

5. Religious liberties were intended to apply to   T   F
Judeo-Christian groups, and should not be equally
extended to cults and other religions.

6. The free exercise of religion protects one from   T   F
performing any act against religious convictions.

7. Churches ought to vigorously resist being included   T   F
in the Social Security system.

8. Christian social programs such as day care centers   T   F
or schools ought to comply with the same regulations as
non-Christian programs so long as it doesn't prevent them
from teaching their faith.

9. Laws ought to be passed to prevent cults from   T   F
seeking to influence children.

10. The separation of church and state ought to bar   T   F
religious groups and leaders from taking public positions
on controversial political questions.

* * * * *

A casual Sunday in front of the television would hardly create the impression that our religious liberty is threatened. Every imaginable kind of religious thought is offered, or perhaps more accurately, sold. A trip to an airport likewise may find you assaulted with religious liberty. Your mailbox signals the determination, if not vitality, of religious groups. Could religious liberty be really at stake?

Yet not since the debates in the early 1960s about school prayer have issues of religious liberty been so hotly debated. And the rhetoric is tough. The October 1983 issue of a nationally distributed church paper, *Temple Times,* insisted that the federal government and the states "have wantonly disregarded and trammeled upon the religious liberty of churches, religious organizations, and individuals." Citing the recent expansion of the Social Security system to cover churches, the newsletter insists that "the government now claims sovereign ownership and control of every church in America."

In September 1983, the American Coalition of Unregistered Churches was founded, indicating it will provide resources on constitutional rights for churches and give legal assistance "whenever the crest of the wave of tyranny breaks."

Cases recently before the Supreme Court have elicited strong comment. Cases such as *Bob Jones University vs. U.S.* (Can the IRS deny tax-exemption to BJU based on its failure to comply with public policy regarding racial policies?) and *Lynch vs. Donnelly* (Can a city own and display a manger scene on public property as part of a larger Christmas annual display?) are monitored carefully for signs of further erosion.

What is going on? Is Old Glory going down the drain?

Clashing Institutions

From one perspective, this is a clash between major interests and institutions. Church and state have always been powerful institutions, not only in America, but in world history. And today both have substantially grown. Churches today are aggressive. Churches are involved in education, social service, relief efforts, entertainment, television, and even certain businesses. Ministers are now administrators and TV personalities.

Likewise, the scope of government is growing almost exponentially. The regulatory activities of state and federal agencies extend into almost every area of life.

It is no wonder these institutions bump into one another. Both of them are also legitimate institutions from a biblical perspective. But to complete the picture, we ought to add one other institution—the family. These three institutions are ordained by God and serve specific social and spiritual purposes. The church's central missions are to proclaim the Gospel, baptize, ordain, nurture and equip the saints, and serve as a prophetic check on the government.

The government's primary responsibilities are to restrain evil, reward good, secure civil peace, and advance public justice. The family provides a structure for the procreation and nurture of children, the linkage to our larger communal responsibilities, and a place of identity and responsibility.

The interests of these three institutions inevitably intersect. It is at the points of interaction that many of today's clashes occur. Some clashes represent inappropriate claims of one institution which would improperly diminish the role of another. Other times, it seems less clear where the lines ought to be drawn. As a society we must work out, in a political context, the balance of these roles.

While the church is an institution which competes and is separate from the "state," the same is not true of "religion." Religion, both in a sociological as well as a Christian sense, is not an institution, rather it is a set of perspectives, values, and commitments which is not limited to the "church," but extends into all of life. One is a Christian (or a Moslem or a Mormon) not simply in the sphere of the church, but in family and state relationships as well. This is a critical distinction because the notion that religion can or ought to be separate is recognized as impossible and even ill-advised.

Historically, church and state (less so the family) have clashed, and a variety of models describe their proper relationship. Four general options have emerged.

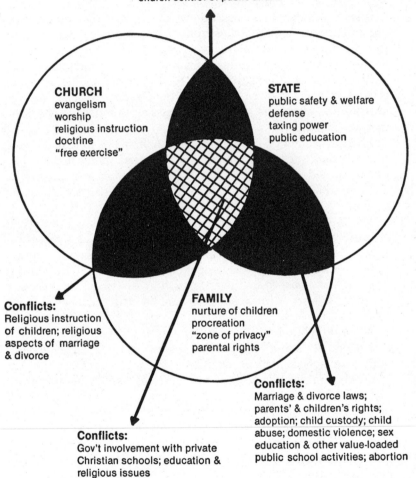

Conflicts:
Gov't regulation of churches;
e.g., licenses, taxes, zoning,
employment practices, fund-
raising regulation, limits on
church control of public affairs

CHURCH
evangelism
worship
religious instruction
doctrine
"free exercise"

STATE
public safety & welfare
defense
taxing power
public education

Conflicts:
Religious instruction
of children; religious
aspects of marriage
& divorce

FAMILY
nurture of children
procreation
"zone of privacy"
parental rights

Conflicts:
Marriage & divorce laws;
parents' & children's rights;
adoption; child custody; child
abuse; domestic violence; sex
education & other value-loaded
public school activities; abortion

Conflicts:
Gov't involvement with private
Christian schools; education &
religious issues

These circles show the major interests of three "institutions" of
American life. The conflicts arise where these three intersect.

The separationist model. Some contend the best model to assure the integrity of each sphere is a total separation between church and state. Some would suggest the family also ought to have a totally separate sphere of authority, independent from the state. Some secularists hold to such a separation because they do not want the state corrupted by religion. Some Christians advocate this because they fear the state will corrupt the church, or the state will favor some particular expression of the church. People who think government is evil will call for total separation because they want nothing to do with the state. They want to be left alone. They insist the church is not subject at all to the civil authority.

Such a theory is easy to graph, but impossible to implement. Since family, state, and church are all on the same turf and have the same subjects, interaction is inevitable. Churches own property, families pay taxes, children are baptized and educated. And even if it were possible to create airtight separation, it would be tragic if these institutions did not interact—for they would not be able to teach each other, challenge each other, and limit each other's excesses.

The triumphant church. Throughout history some have believed that God intended for the church to be society's primary authority. American history has had times when the church was absolutely or nearly dominant. Most of the colonies established state churches with tax support. Massachusetts had a state tax supported church till 1933! Dissenters were frequently run out. Colonial preachers and religious leaders were often the actual or *de facto* leaders. For many years, New Hampshire required all elected state officials to be Protestants, and Maryland required a belief in God till 1961. Laws in some areas barred non-Christians from serving as legal witnesses and from voting.

Attempting to fulfill the Great Commission with political clout poses a great temptation. The record of the spiritual vitality of such politically dominant bodies is not altogether impressive. Political authority combined with a religious sanction too often corrupts the spiritual mission of the church and creates an intolerant church.

The dominant state. A more familiar pattern shows the state dominating the church and family with an iron fist. The state has the soldiers and guns. The state has the law. The state may also have the power of communication.

When the state exercises this sort of authority, the result is tyranny. The Roman Empire, Nazi Germany, and dictatorships of both the left and the right are prime examples. In Soviet states, the family serves the state. Any interest in family autonomy is seen as a capitalist, anti-state act. The chief crime in Soviet societies is to be "anti-state" because the state represents the will of the people.

The dangers of such a state increase as state power expands, especially where the government's power is enhanced with technological strengths in communications, finance, and education. It was such a fear that produced George Orwell's *1984* and Aldous Huxley's *Brave New World.* In these prophetic novels, the dominant state is all-pervasive. It does not think of itself as tyrannical, but as "modern," "efficient," and serving the public good. It is this sort of dominant state—the one with a messianic notion— that is the most dangerous. This type of government not only wants your obedience, it wants your worship too.

Separate, yet intersecting and interacting. This perspective recognizes that there are separate functions and roles for the three entities, and each must have a substantial measure of autonomy to properly fulfill its role. But this view reflects the need for interaction between these spheres. For example, both the church and the family are to be involved in nurturing believers and equipping the saints. In areas such as tax exemptions and relief efforts, both the state and the church are interacting. There are also some areas in which no sphere has an ultimate monopoly. In matters such as education, justice, and human life, all three institutions have strong interests.

The debate about church and state and religious liberty is really a question of authority and responsibility. Our position on conflicts between church and state will be shaped by which sphere we believe has primary responsibility for that activity.

The philosophic battle over spheres of authority is not in the abstract. Rather these struggles occur in specific contexts. While the total scope of these conflicts is enormous, a few recurring areas are worth noting.

Is the Court Doing Us In?

A recurring complaint of many is that the government and specifically our courts are responsible for a dramatic shift in the relationship of Christian values and ideals to modern society. As Senator Sam Ervin put it the day after the Supreme Court's 1962 decision banning school prayers, "The Supreme Court today has made God unconstitutional."

Has the Supreme Court shattered the historic affirmation of Christian principles on which our nation was founded? Has it forced upon the nation a vision of America contrary to both the dreams of the founders and aspirations of our citizens?

While there are debates about precisely how religious America was in the early days of our nation, there is no doubt that Christian principles were at the foundation of our national life. When the framers of the Constitution wrote the First Amendment provision that "Congress shall make no law respecting an establishment of religion," they barred a state church for the new nation. But the notion of a secular state was far from their minds. If they had wished to isolate religion from the state, they would not have set up a chaplain system for Congress. Nor would they have called on the President to establish a national day of "public thanksgiving and prayer, to be observed by acknowledging with grateful hearts, the many signal favors of the Almighty God." Congress even authorized the provision of federal funds for religious proselytization and education among Indians.

The Christian faith's central role in America continued to modern times. The phrase "under God" was added to the Pledge of Allegiance by congressional amendment in 1954; "In God we trust" was placed on our coins in 1955.

So comfortable was the loose Christian consensus that the Supreme Court did not even decide a case about the Constitution's Establishment Clause till 1947 in *Everson vs. Board of Education.* The Court, for the first time, sought to interpret the meaning of the phrase, "Congress shall make no law respecting an establishment of religion." Though the decision upheld a state law providing reimbursement for transportation costs, the historic aspect of the decision was its declaration: "The First Amendment has erected a wall between church and state. That wall must be kept high and impregnable. We could not approve the slightest breach."

The Court's decision and subsequent cases based on the concept of a "wall of separation" seem to have significantly altered the relationship between religion and the state. Official school prayers were barred in 1962 (*Engel vs. Vitale*) as was compulsory Bible reading in 1963 (*Abington vs. Schempp*). Numerous decisions barred federal and state financial aid to parochial schools except in the most limited way. In 1981 the Court barred the posting of the Ten Commandments in the classrooms of Kentucky (*Stone vs. Graham*). Religious instructions of students in the school, even if by non-school personnel with parents' permission, was also held unconstitutional (*McCollum vs. Board of Education*). Lower courts have struck down silent meditation statutes, barred Christmas manger scenes on public property, and barred Christian groups from meeting before school for prayer.

The Court pointed to the nation's founders to justify those decisions. But their reading of history was surely skewed. When they noted that our society had largely changed, and once acceptable practices were now controversial, they seemed correct. But debates will continue to rage about the proper degree of separation between church and state. Many, however, believe the Court in the 60s went to questionable extremes in its erection of a "high and impregnable wall of separation." Not only was such a view unhistorical, it created the potential for abuse.

But lest we think that the Supreme Court is always the villain, we should note several moderating factors. First, American society now is simply not the same as it was in the colonial period. Not only are there many people with no religious interests whatever, but our nation's religious diversity has broadened. It is increasingly difficult, for example, to think even of a generalized prayer which would find support between the various religious groups.

The Court may have erred in seeking to defend the separation principle on the intent of the framers, but some forms of separation may be an appropriate response to a changed society.

Second, the decisions which created the most controversy are not as odious as is often charged. In *Engel* and *Abington,* the Court declared that schools and teachers are not to compose prayers or become priests and ministers for students. In *McCollum,* the Court in effect held that sectarian religious education is the business of homes and churches and not the business of the schools. These are only seen as revolutionary decisions because of the long customs of such practices. But in principle, Christians could hardly contend that they represented a fundamental assault on religion.

Third, the Court has often been a vigorous defender of religious liberty. In 1972 the Supreme Court barred Wisconsin from compelling the Amish to send their children to high school against their conscience and religious convictions (*Wisconsin vs. Yoder*); and in 1963 the Court held that unemployment benefits could not be denied a worker because, out of religious convictions about working on the Sabbath, she had lost her job (*Sherbert vs. Verner*). The Court has also determined that schools must accommodate the religious beliefs of students and allow them to be dismissed for a regular weekly period to attend religious instruction classes (*Zorach vs. Clausen*); that the National Labor Relations Board could not exercise jurisdiction over religious schools (*NLRB vs. Catholic Bishops*); that university authorities may not discriminate against religious students who wish to meet on campus for worship (*Widmar vs. Vincent*); that a state may employ and utilize a state legislative chaplain (*Marsh vs. Chambers*); and that a state may not discriminate among religious groups in legislation concerning solicitation of funds (*Larsen vs. Valente*).

While the tendency to overuse the establishment clause to especially burden religion or radically segregate religion and morals from the state is a serious threat, it is also a serious injustice to see the Supreme Court as an implacable foe of religious freedom. In fact, the Court has often defended religious diversity against attempts by other government agencies, such as zoning boards, state legislatures, tax authorities, and school officials to limit or discriminate against religion.

The Supreme Court's decisions in no way reflect a basic hostility to religious expression. The changes in the moral and spiritual tone of our society are rooted in more fundamental aspects than a few court decisions. The failure of the church, the extreme hedonism and materialism of our society, and the philosophic loss of a commitment to ultimate truths are the real sources of our spiritual decline. The Court makes a convenient scapegoat, but its decision about school prayer hardly is responsible for our angst.

Putting the Squeeze On

The Court's interpretation of the Establishment Clause to bar government support for religion has been controversial, but does not seem to impose a great threat to the vitality of religion. Many argue that faith will thrive more vigorously and prophetically when free of any government subsidy.

Who would have thought, though, that the protections of the First Amendment could be used to attempt to force a city to take a drawing of a church off its city parking sticker; to require a state to revise its official seal which contains religious language; to cause a church to lose a tax exemption for activities on abortion issues; or to deny religious students the same rights to meet as others? All of these have been asserted. Somehow a constitutional *liberty* has threatened to become an *impediment*. Extreme applications of the doctrine of separation of church and state would indeed seriously threaten religious liberty and must be vigorously resisted.

When courts require a school like Mumford High in Detroit to officially recognize a student socialist club, the Mumford Young Socialist Union, but declare that the Establishment Clause bars a voluntary prayer meeting at Guiderland High School in Albany—something seems strange. Similarly, when homosexual student Aaron Fricke at Cumberland High School in Rhode Island obtains a court order requiring the school to let him attend the prom with his "date" Paul, but the American Civil Liberties

Union successfully stops the Lubbock School District from permitting religious students to meet at the school before the buses arrive—something seems amiss. How can a court compel a school to permit the distribution of a counterculture newspaper by nonstudents on the campus, citing free speech of the Constitution, but other courts bar distribution of Bibles by Gideons? How is it a court protects what many see as vulgar books often used in school curriculums, but bars the posting of the Ten Commandments? Maybe those decisions make sense, but at first blush they appear to represent a peculiar kind of neutrality.

In many cases, the Establishment Clause has become a legal rationale to silence the church in terms of any public affairs. Many who believe that the church ought to stay out of running the government also think that the church should stay out of any comment on public life or engagement with society. Put otherwise, this view says religion ought to "stay in its place."

This is precisely the way separation of church and state works in the Soviet Union. There is a measure, however small, of religious liberty. But the liberty only extends to the theoretical (often denied in practice) right to worship—i.e., pray, listen to sermons, and sing. The church and believers are barred from any participation in debates about public policy, in offering humanitarian services such as food relief and welfare, or involvement in education.

In this extreme form, religion is not merely prevented from receiving special aid, but is positively discriminated against because it is religious. Instead of the government being neutral, the government affirmatively discriminates against religion. In several cases in the United States, a few courts have rendered decisions which reflect this hostility to religion.

In *McRae vs. Califano* the plaintiffs sought to invalidate the Hyde Amendment which prohibited the use of federal funds for abortion. They argued such a bar was unconstitutional because it reflected a viewpoint advanced by religion.

In two U.S. federal district courts, trial judges held that the Establishment Clause *required* state universities to bar religious student groups from meeting at campus facilities. Other student groups were allowed, even encouraged, but these courts said religious students were not entitled to the same rights because they wanted to speak about religious matters. (*Chess vs. Widmar, Dittman vs. Western Washington University.*) This position was definitely rejected by the Supreme Court in *Widmar vs. Vincent*, where its 8-1 decision barred such discrimination.

This hostile mentality was also evidenced by the American Bar Association's initial decision to deny accreditation to the law school at Oral Roberts University. There were also some doubts initially about whether graduates of Falwell's Liberty Baptist College could receive state teacher's licenses since Liberty taught creationism.

The same pressure is seen in attempts to squeeze the moral views of religious persons out of the public sector on the grounds that they are religious in character. When the notion of separation of church and state devolves into the separation of morals and the state, our whole culture is threatened. Yet traditional moral views about sexuality are often totally ignored in public school classes, partly because those views would intrude religious values into the state's educational program. Textbooks which may express values related to religion are likewise suspect, while, of course, texts which advocate secular viewpoints are hailed.

These trends reflect more than government neutrality. They reflect a denigration of the role of religious institutions and moral discourse in our public lives. Legitimate concepts of separation of church and state intended to shield improper entanglements must not become swords by which some can silence our religious elements.

Since government controls and involvements are steadily expanding, any perspective which requires church and religious views to be silent wherever government is present will steadily shrink the witness of believers. A failure to be open and neutral creates an arbitrary "load" or bias in all public activities—a bias in favor of views that do not use religious words or are not derived from obviously religious institutions. To exclude religion on the grounds of neutrality is a myth. We are not treating something neutrally when one major and historic branch of thought is held suspect.

Such a view runs counter to our historic commitment to a vital relationship between religion and public life. Only a serious misreading of the Establishment Clause or a deliberate hostility to religious values and institutions can sustain a legal posture which advocates an absolute separation between church and state.

5

Limits on Government Interference with Religion

Heinrich is a deeply religious believer in God. He belongs to a small community of believers that have lived in rural North Dakota for four generations. They have avoided participating in the larger society, eschewed politics, and carried on their agrarian way of life.

Many would call them old-fashioned—and they don't mind the label. Heinrich more than once had told townsfolk that if "new fashioned" meant the sort of violence and family disintegration he saw among them, he was proud to be weird.

Now, however, there is trouble. Heinrich refuses to get a driver's license because it would have his picture on it, and he believes that would violate a biblical command to have no graven image. Nor will he buy license plates for his tractors. He says the phrase on the plates, "A Great Nation," is idolatrous.

When he was ticketed for driving his tractor, his defense was that the statutes violate his religious liberty, and specifically they violate the First Amendment's clause which bars government from any act prohibiting the free exercise of religion.

What do you think? Why?

* * * * *

In May 1983 the United States Supreme Court rendered its decision in *Bob Jones University vs. United States*. The case had generated strong opinions and presented to the Court several sensitive issues: racism, religious liberty, and taxation.

Bob Jones University opposed racial intermarriage on religious grounds. Though the University had once barred all blacks from admission, its policies had shifted in recent years. By 1980 the policy of admissions was non-discriminatory, but there were bars on interracial dating and interracial marriage.

Enter the Internal Revenue Service. The IRS, noting these practices, revoked the tax-exemption of the University. According to the IRS, BJU's racial practices were violative of public policy and hence BJU was not entitled to tax-exemption. BJU filed suit alleging that this revocation violated, among other things, the guarantees of free exercise of religion by placing a special impediment in the way of those who practiced their religious faith as BJU did.

The U.S. district court agreed and held that the denial of exemption was impermissible. The judge held that to use "public policy" grounds as a basis for denying tax-exemption would exert pressure on all religious groups to "stay in step" with official government views. On appeal, however, a 2-1 majority reversed and upheld the denial of exemption. The case was appealed to the Supreme Court.

The case was a strange one in many ways. The Reagan administration had officially sided against the IRS not so much on constitutional grounds as on the grounds that Congress had not authorized the IRS to deny exemption on such grounds. Congress couldn't seem to get any concensus. Then there were the strange bedfellows—fundamentalist and evangelical organizations were joined by some of the most liberal groups in the country, including the National Council of Churches, in raising serious warnings about any policy that allowed the use of tax power to punish or reward particular religious viewpoints.

Few were eager to defend the actual policies of BJU, but the legal principles were of potential momentous proportions: may the IRS, on the basis of its assessment of public policy, deny tax-exemption to groups which do not conform their views and practices to those public policies? Some believed that such a position opened the door to great abuse, deeply entangling government with the sincere beliefs of religious groups. They wondered what other "public policies" were likely to be the basis for denial of exemption. Would all religious groups that practice discrimination on the basis of sex, such as the Roman Catholic Church in its ordination practices, now lose their exemption? What about resistance to policies opposing discrimination on the basis of sexual preference?

The Supreme Court's decision was not close. By an 8-1 margin, the Court sustained the denial of exemption. The Court held that tax-exemptions have historically been based on the concept that the exempt body is "charitable." As such, there is a right to expect that these "charities" not engage in practices fundamentally antithetical to the public interest. The majority opinion required that "an institution seeking tax-exempt status must serve a public purpose and not be contrary to established public policy."

What about free exercise? The Court admitted the practices of BJU were based on sincerely held religious beliefs. But in a brief analysis of two paragraphs, the Court rejected any claim that there was a violation of the rights of free exercise of religion. The Court held two things: first, there was not a genuine infringement of belief and practice since there was no bar to BJU continuing its practices. The decision was only a refusal to provide the "benefit" of tax-exemption. Second, there was a compelling state interest, an overwhelmingly important issue, that of racial discrimination which is a clear public policy of the United States. Thus BJU lost.

The concurring opinion of Justice Potter Stewart seemed to recognize what many saw as the potential danger. He warned against the rationale of the majority. Stewart suggested that there may be great public interest in NOT seeking to compel all tax-exempt groups to conform to the party line. Diversity in organizations is important to the political dialogue in the nation and there is danger in requiring all tax exempt groups to fit the public policy test.

The decision does seem to reflect a new basis for tax-exemption.

But we should realize that the Court, in a footnote to the opinion, noted that this case did not involve a church or "purely religious organization," but a school. The Court suggested that educational institutions have a greater responsibility to reflect the public policies than do purely religious organizations.

Many have viewed the BJU decision as representing a serious threat to religious freedom. Is "free exercise" in danger?

Free Exercise: The Concept

The Constitution's First Amendment clearly protects religious liberty and specifically bars government interference. The First Amendment not only prohibits the "establishment of religion," but also puts another limit on government: "Nor prohibiting the free exercise thereof." The first clause prohibits government sponsorship or advocacy of religion. The second prevents the government from interfering with religious "exercise."

But as firm as these prohibitions sound, it is not hard to imagine that they have not always been easy to apply. What does the Constitution mean by free "exercise"? And what qualifies as "religion"?

Protecting Belief, Not Action

In an early case which first applied the Free Exercise Clause, *Reynolds vs. United States* (1878), the Supreme Court held that the free execise clause protects religious *belief* absolutely, but does not protect all religious *conduct*. While the government "cannot interfere with mere religious belief and opinion, they may with practices." Thus Reynolds, who claimed a free exercise right to practice polygamy in accord with his religious beliefs, even though it was against the law, was not successful.

Reynolds makes clear there are limits to free exercise. Some basic policies are so central to our way of life that regardless of how religiously based our claims are, we will not be granted exemption.

It wasn't long, however, till the Court recognized that more than mere belief was protected by the First Amendment. In 1940 in *Cantwell vs. Connecticut,* the Court, in reversing the conviction of Cantwell for proselytization efforts in the city streets, declared: "The amendment embraces two concepts—freedom to believe and freedom to act." Free exercise meant more than belief. It included some action—not all, but some. Thus the stage was set for the determining of which "acts" are protected, and which are not.

As our society has become more diverse religiously, these issues have become more complex. With the infusion into our society of new religious groups, a variety of cults, and some very questionable organizations seeking to operate under the label of religion, the courts have been faced with much more difficult questions of free exercise. As people become more sensitive to the clashes between government policies and their religious faith, the clashes increase. For example, in recent years courts have faced such questions as:

Can a school prohibit the wearing of yarmulkes by basketball players?

Should native Americans be prosecuted for using peyote in their religious worship services?

Can prisons require persons with religious beliefs about long hair to have their hair cut?

Can airports bar religious persons from soliciting for contributions in the facilities?

Over the years, an analytical process has developed by which the Court reviews whether a given claim of religious liberty will succeed. Here, somewhat oversimplified, is the test:

1. Has the state/government *burdened* the exercise of a *sincerely* held *religious* belief?

2. If so, is there a sufficiently *compelling state interest* to justify this interference?

3. And if so, has the government in implementing its legitimate compelling interests, used the *least intrusive means* possible so that the infringement on religious exercise is the minimal necessary to achieve its legitimate interests?

But such verbal tests don't have all the answers. They only identify the important issues.

Substantial Protections

Often the courts have been sensitive to religious liberty/free exercise claims and protected them against government intrusion. Beginning with *Cantwell vs. Connecticut* in 1940, the courts have often barred intrusive government regulations and prohibitions. Often these protections have come in decisions concerning unpopular religious groups.

Key victories for religious liberty are usually based on free exercise protections. Religious liberty is, however, also often based on the protections of free speech and equal protection. Among the strong Supreme Court protections are the following:

Pierce vs. Society of Sisters (1925): Struck down attempts to compel parents to send their children to public schools.

Cantwell vs. Connecticut (1940): Struck down a statute requiring a license for solicitating and which gave an official broad discretion on whether to grant such a permit or not.

Martin vs. Struthers (1943): A town could not ban distribution of literature door to door. Nor may a permit for religious meetings be denied solely because of dislike for the views to be expressed, *Niemotko vs. Maryland* (1943).

West Virginia State Board of Education vs. Barnette (1943): Struck down attempts to compel students against their religious convictions to engage in certain patriotic ceremonies, such as saluting the flag.

Sherbert vs. Verner (1963): Overruled the denial of unemployment benefits to a Seventh Day Adventist who refused to take work that required Sabbath employment as an unconstitutional burden on religious liberty. In this widely cited case, the Court painted in broad strokes the scope of free exercise protections: "Only the gravest abuses, endangering paramount interests, give occasion for permissible limitation."

People vs. Woody (1964): The state's interest in controlling peyote was not compelling enough to sustain criminal convictions of native Americans for using the substance as part of their religious worship. (But this exemption is narrow. Timothy Leary failed to win a free exercise exemption for narcotics law violations which he alleged were in the context of a recent conversion to a religion which used marijuana.)

Wisconsin vs. Yoder (1972): Held that the free exercise rights of

Amish parents were paramount to the state's interest in the compulsory attendance of high school students.

McDaniel vs. Paty (1978): A Tennessee statute barring ministers from serving in the state legislature was held unconstitutional as a violation of the free exercise of religion.

Thomas vs. Review Board (1981): An employee who quit a job rather than engage in employment in a company which made armaments, contrary to his religious beliefs, was exempt from the usual rule which precluded benefits where a person voluntarily quits. Here in strong language the Court protected free exercise:

> When the state conditions receipt of an important benefit upon conduct prescribed by religious faith, or when it denies such a benefit because of conduct mandated by religious belief, thereby putting substantial pressure on an adherent to modify his behavior and to violate his belief, a burden on religion exists.

These decisions reflect a vigorous defense of religious liberty and pluralism. Notice that the "burden on free exercise" arises not only where the government action is *intended* to interfere or even where the interference is *direct*. Unintentional and indirect burdens on religion are also impermissible unless the state shows a compelling interest.

Of course, the protection is not absolute and free exercise rights are not always found compelling. In 1961 the Court rejected a free exercise claim by Orthodox Jews seeking to hold unconstitutional a Sunday Closing Law (*Braunfield vs. Brown*). More recently in *United States vs. Lee* (1982) the Court held that the Amish were not entitled under the Free Exercise Claim to an exemption from social security taxes.

Sometimes the claim of free exercise violations will fail because the Court will reject the sincerity of the religious claim, as perhaps in the *Leary* case noted earlier. Or the Court may accept the sincerity of belief, but argue that the government's acts really don't infringe on that belief; or that there is an infringement, but the state's interests outweigh the religious liberty interest.

If the Court has generally protected free exercise and has what appears to be a reasonable test, why are so many people concerned? Some recent decisions by various courts have created widespread concern. First, there is alarm over the decreased effectiveness of such claims in the face of expanding government activity. As government expands its zone of control, it claims a "compelling interest" in more and more arenas. Second, the courts seem to give less credence to religious liberty claims now than in earlier cases (such as *Sherbert* and *Yoder*). Organizations seem especially vulnerable. The legal system seems much more attune to providing exemptions for individuals such as Adelle Sherbert than recognizing the legitimacy of free exercise interests of institutions. Today these concerns rest in four key areas.

1. Tax power. The use of tax power in the context of religious organizations has drawn substantial attention. The National Council of Churches, under the leadership of Dean Kelly, is engaged in a long-term study on the use of tax power and its impact on churches. The taxing issues are broad, ranging from denial of federal exemption to attempts to deny property tax-exemption to religious organizations. In a New York case, state authorities sought to revoke the property tax-exemption of properties of the Unification Church in New York. The basis for the denial was the public statements of church officials on international and public affairs. Deep concern was expressed in many religious communities that the use of tax power to limit the issues about which churches could speak was especially dangerous. A New York Court of Appeals finally reversed the local taxing authority.

Investigations of churches by the IRS have at times seemed excessive. As a result, federal legislation (the Church Audit Procedures Act) has been introduced to avoid some of the excesses. One church subjected to IRS investigation was ultimately given a clean bill of health, but spent over $70,000 in legal fees to establish its rights.

2. The "public trust" theory. In 1980 the State of California applied a "public trust" theory to religious organizations. The state declared that the assets of a religious corporation should be held in trust; it is the state's duty to assure that the funds are used properly. In a case involving the Worldwide Church of God, the state court appointed a receiver that actually controlled the funds of the church and took administrative control of the church's affairs, including deciding whether the church's leader could send out certain pastoral letters. This was without any specific finding of wrongdoing! Only subsequent legislation terminated the interference.

Unpopular religious groups seem frequently singled out for restrictions under what appear to be neutral and reasonable state schemes, but which often are designed to target specific groups. Statutes have been introduced in many states to permit persons to gain legal custody of adults who have come under the influence of what opponents believe are dangerous "cult" groups. Such statutes are frequently nothing but assaults on the whole notion of religious conversion, and could be applied as equally to Christianity.

3. *General government regulation.* Another area of interference is in the application of government regulations to religious organizations and ministries. Federal and state agencies play an increasing role in licensing and supervising activities and organizations. Such regulations and supervision are common in such areas of labor relations (employment practices), zoning regulations, and various public services (such as day care centers, public and private education, relief work, etc.).

These regulations pose difficult constitutional questions. When does a regulation interfere with the exercise of religion? And when it does, is there a compelling state interest? Does the regulation reflect the least intrusive means for the state to achieve its interests? At issue is not simply the Free Exercise Clause, but often the prohibition against the entanglement of government with religion. This "entanglement" prohibition is part of the Court's understanding of the Establishment Clause. Obviously any regulation constitutes some measure of entanglement, but how much is too much—or to use the Court's terms, when is it "excessive"? When does state regulation of ministries constitute an impermissible violation of the free exercise of religion?

4. *Intrusion into value arena of Christian organizations.* An increasingly urgent issue is the tendency of government agencies and some lower courts to show little awareness of the value systems and moral beliefs that are the bases of many religious

organizations and ministries. As government regulations and supervision expand, the clashes with religious liberty become more frequent.

A realtor in Virginia was required by a federal agency to stop using a Christian symbol on the company's stationery and cards, and was required to advertise in several papers his nondiscriminatory policies. The agency had decided that advertising one's Christianity was implicit discrimination.

A reporter for the *Christian Science Monitor* alleged that she was fired because she would not submit to counseling regarding her homosexual orientation and called it impermissible discrimination. A prominent religious radio station in the Northwest was told that it could not use a religious factor in hiring on the air announcers for its radio programs. A private club in Minnesota is on trial for allegedly violating the Minnesota Human Rights Act by promoting "born-again growing Christians" to management positions.

Church-operated schools, orphanages, and hospitals may be challenged because of the advocacy of certain moral and spiritual commitments inherent in their faith. Private citizens may increasingly find that their moral persuasions are seen by the government as "discrimination," as for example where a court may bar a landlord from declining to rent to unmarried couples or to a homosexual couple.

While the elimination of racial discrimination is a worthy goal, the government's tendency to use the label "discrimination" against those who exercise important moral judgments is dangerous. Choosing, discriminating, and rejecting are central aspects of mature decision-making. They are also at the heart of religious and moral commitments.

Conclusion

These complex areas represent troublesome arenas of government threat to free exercise. The burden is often indirect and unintentional; but for that very reason, it poses a danger that under the guise of "neutral" and social welfare commitments, the independence of religious life will be diminished. Courts do seem sensitive to rights of free exercise, but they must be challenged to see that these rights encompass more than individual rights of worship; they include moral principles and institutional life as well.

Warning!
As critical as religious liberty defense is, watch out. There are several areas where we must exercise caution.

1. Is it really religious liberty? Not every interference with religious expression is an assault on religious liberty. When a church declares that it ought to be exempt from using the grade of steel for its church building which ordinances require, it has confused religious liberty with mere expense. Religious liberty protections do not guarantee that the exercise of faith is without any restriction or inconvenience.

2. Even bureaucrats are people! Attacks on government policy too often are couched in language and fought in styles which imply that government and all its employees are engaged in a massive evil conspiracy. But this is not true.

It's not hard to pick a fight. A rebellious and cantankerous spirit can almost always create a battle which can be billed as a fight for freedom. There are times, to be sure, when it will be necessary to marshal legal resources and do battle for the protection of spiritual liberties. But those times must be carefully chosen.

We must also recognize that Scripture indicates that government is a gift of God (see John 19:10-11). And in a democracy we have a special opportunity to shape the character of our laws and policies. We are the government.

3. "You were faithful with a few things" (Matt. 25:23, NASB). Christians are much more energetic in fighting for theoretical rights than they are in exercising the rights they have. If Christians prayed with their children at home as consistently as they complained that schoolteachers couldn't, our society would be different. Scripture teaches that gifts not exercised, opportunities not claimed will result in withdrawn gifts (see Matt. 25:14-30). We have substantial religious liberties of evangelism, use of media and literature, and worship is almost totally unrestricted. Use it or lose it!

4. *Know your rights.* Christians rarely know their legal rights. A teacher may be told it is unconstitutional to have a Bible in the classroom. A youth group may be told they can't distribute literature in a city park because it litters the grounds. School officials may avoid singing any religious music at a Christmas program at the school because they believe it's not permitted. Yet they would all be wrong. It is time to learn the scope of our religious liberties. (Refer to the authors' book, *The Battle for Religious Liberty,* David C. Cook Publishing Co., for more on this subject.)

5. *"Fret not"* (Prov. 24:19). We must remain confident in God's sovereignty and thankful to Him. Scripture warns us not to fret over evildoers (Ps. 37:1, 7-8). We are to give thanks, even in situations of suffering and trouble. A bitter and resentful spirit will create neither liberty nor joy. What is the point of liberty or winning our rights if we lose both our witness and our joy in Christ? Rights are important, but we must be cautious lest we fall into a secularist trap—an inordinate focus on rights. Thankfulness, obedience, and trust are the marks of believers—not our defense of our rights.

6. *Consistency—what's good for the goose. . . .* We often view rights as something that Christians ought to have (because we are right) but that others should not have (because they are wrong). Many would quite willingly allow legal restrictions on what they see as "cults" or peculiar groups. But religious liberties are a seamless web, not divisible. It is essential to defend those liberties at their first attack. Today, many serious issues of religious liberty involve groups such as the Worldwide Church of God or the Unification Church. As strange as their theologies may be, or as bizarre as we may view their practices, we must vigorously assure for them the same rights we wish for ourselves. If we fail, the principles will be lost for all of us.

7. *It's not hopeless.* One principle has repeatedly been demonstrated. Carefully framed arguments or cases may secure great liberties. But bad cases make bad laws.

When the rights of Christian students were being denied at

colleges and universities across the country, a well-planned case was developed in Missouri to win an important right—the right of Christian student groups to meet and speak on campuses just as other student groups did. An 8-1 decision of the Supreme Court secured that fundamental right.

It is not so important how many cases are filed, or how much noise you make. The key is to establish basic principles, and you only need to win one case to do that (if it is the right case in the right place). Careful planning makes the difference.

8. Don't believe everything you hear. You'd better check the facts when you hear or read of some great threat to liberty. It happens again and again. Remember the flap about Proctor and Gamble's logo being demonic? Or the persistent rumor the FCC was going to bar religious programming? Then there's a story about a public school teacher in a northern plains state who was fired for teaching about Creation.

Our credibility in the professional communities of law, politics, and education is at stake. Let's get the facts right.

6

Pornography and the Law

Under the guise of liberty, freedom, and human development we are witnessing an increasing degradation of human dignity and the loss of liberty and culture. Pornography is one manifestation of this liberty and license run amok. Live sex shows, massage parlors, and "rent a girl" escort services at national political conventions are among the louder samples. Softer, but equally attune to the spirit of the age, are those television programs, films, and books which glorify marital infidelity, seek to make sexual liberation a great personal achievement, and ridicule traditional family and sexual values.

Pornography is now big business, creating revenue estimated at $4 billion a year—more than the legitimate motion picture and record industries. Virtually the entire pornography industry is centralized and controlled by organized crime interests.

Yet a congressional study by the Commission on Obscenity and Pornography showed only 2 percent of the public believe that pornography is one of the major issues facing our society. Either we have bought the idea that freedom of expression includes pornography (who wants censors?), or we don't understand the character of contemporary pornography (what's wrong with sex?), or we are indifferent to the questions of how people choose to entertain themselves (it's nobody's business).

Full-fledged pornography businesses are booming. *Deep Throat,* described by a judge as "Sodom and Gomorrah gone wild," became the first mass distributed porno film. Pornographic magazines are sold by chain bookstores and grocery stores across the nation. The biggest seller of pornography of all, some suggest, is Southland Corporation's 7-Eleven stores.

Pin-ups are no longer the issue. William Stanmeyer, in testimony before the U.S. House of Representatives, said:

> We are talking about something so hideous and barbaric that people who have not seen it cannot believe it exists, that people who have seen it grope for euphemisms to water down its vileness, and that people who indulge their morbid fantasies with it do so furtively, wearing dark glasses as they enter the "adult" bookstore.

Reo M. Christenson, political scientist, wrote in *The Cincinnati Enquirer,* "Those appalled by the prospect of censorship usually do not realize what they are protecting. Or what, through postal subsidies, they help distribute." Writing specifically of *Hustler,* Christenson declared, "It is not a 'girlie' magazine. . . . Rather it is full of pictures of such gross sexual perversion, such forms of bestiality and such nauseating accounts of excretory activities that few if any newspapers feel free to explicitly inform their readers of what is in the magazine."

A Silent People

Yet few people really seem concerned. Most are willing to live and let live. A few organizations such as Citizens for Decency Through Law, Morality in Media, and Coalition for Better Television have sought to inform and rally individuals to use their moral and economic power to call for higher values. But most are merely saddened and silent.

Perhaps some people are afraid of being labeled a "censor"— one of those grim-faced prudes. After all, this is "adult" literature, and who wants to be childish?

Opponents of any controls raise specters of book burners, give great publicity to the most extreme groups, and hail liberty and the Constitution. The American Civil Liberties Union has even sought to get courts to declare the voluntary rating systems for movies (G, PG, R, X) unconstitutional! The ACLU, at times the pornographers' best friend, filed suit in Illinois to force a city to permit "adult" programming on its cable system.

Shouldn't We Do Something?

Despite the scope of exploding pornography, there are those who advise against any effort to curb it, especially through the law. Most of the arguments against restrictions are not so much a defense of pornography per se, as a criticism of any regulation. One author listed 36 arguments against obscenity legislation, including such reasoning as:

You can't legislate morality.

Obscenity crimes are crimes without victims.

Obscenity laws violate freedom of speech guaranteed by the Constitution.

The real obscenities in life are poverty and war, not sex.

Obscenity is undefinable.

Pornography never hurt anyone.

Who is qualified to be our censor?

Censorship interferes with artistic creativity.

Government ought to stay out of people's private lives.

Obscenity statutes largely reflect moral and religious views which should not have government support.

Those arguments reflect a perspective of radical individualism, the rejection of moral absolutes, and a denial of the right or ability of a society to guard its own values and culture. Most such arguments could just as easily be used to bar pure food and drug legislation, child labor laws, and discrimination legislation.

Is It Harmful?

Opponents of pornography controls frequently declare that it is a "victimless" crime, that no one can prove it harms anyone, so why regulate it? In 1970, a National Commission on Obscenity and Pornography issued a highly controversial report which said there was no evidence that pornography resulted in crime and urged the abolition of laws criminalizing such materials.

Some studies are not so sure and show a significant number of sex crimes that are linked to an immersion in pornography. That does not mean that all persons who view pornographic materials will commit some sex-related crimes, nor that one may make easy statistical tables which show direct links. But the linkage is by no means surprising. There are compelling reasons to believe that a society satiated with pornography is in fact at serious risk—an immediate risk, but even more critically, a long-term threat.

We ought to totally reject the argument that such literature has no negative impact on the readers. Robert Fitch was surely correct when he observed that "all artists are evangelists." There is a message being communicated. What is the evangelist of pornography selling?

We have no difficulty at all recognizing how attitudes affect conduct. Racist attitudes do lead to discriminatory conduct. Attitudes toward people affect our behavior. Yet somehow we're supposed to believe that pornography has no effect. Nicholas von Hoffman, in an essay "Assault by Film" in the *Washington Post,* noted:

> Why is it liberals, who believe role models in third grade readers are of decisive influence on behavior when it concerns racist or male chauvinist piggery, laugh at the assertion that pornography may also teach rape? . . . If textbooks, those vapid and insipid instruments of such slight influence, can have such sweeping effect, what are we to surmise about the effects on the impressionably young of an R- or X-rated movie, in wide-screen technicolor, with Dolby sound and every device of cinematic realism?

Women's groups are well aware of the attitudes and stereotypes evident in pornography. A magazine article, "Violent Pornography and the Women's Movement," declared, "We think it's harmful in that it contributes to the overall environment that romanticizes, trivializes, and even encourages violence against women."

The anti-female strand is strong in pornography. The ultimate pornographer, Marquis de Sade, saw all women as objects at men's sexual disposal. He said, "We have the right to decree laws that compel women to yield to the flames of him who would have her; violence itself being one of that right's effects, we can employ it lawfully. . . . All men therefore have an equal right of enjoyment of all women."

The psychological impact on our attitudes might well be devastating. As Justice John Harlan noted, "Over a long period of time, the indiscriminate dissemination of materials, the essential character of which is to degrade sex, will have an eroding effect on moral standards."

Freedom or Dehumanizing?

The tragedy is that for all the talk about liberty and self-discovery in sexual license and pornography, the actual result is the loss of any real liberty and the dehumanization of all involved. Pornography abuses persons. Pornography sees persons as things, organs, images. We often forget the underworld of crime and brutality which is the context of much of the pornography today.

The dehumanization of persons involved in the production of pornography is difficult to imagine. The dehumanization has a profound psychological dimension. The radical separation of sexuality from human personality in pornography gives no fulfillment. They entice, but do not satisfy. Like a drug, the demand is for greater and greater stimulation. It is a trap and dead end.

Biblical Perspectives

Specific biblical teachings contain instructions about the nature of our bodies. We are to be careful of the way we use our bodies since they are temples of the Holy Spirit (1 Cor. 6:15-20); we are warned not to conform to the attitudes of the world (Rom. 12:2).

The Bible specifically condemns sexual immorality, which is always at the heart of the images of pornography. Specific sexual perversions common in pornography are directly forbidden (Mark 7:20-23; Rom. 1:24-32; 1 Cor. 6:9-11; Eph. 5:12). We are to put to death indecency and fornication (Col. 3:1, 5).

But the most serious evil in pornography is its treatment of sexuality itself. Sex is God's gift for procreation (Gen. 1:27-28) and for companionship (2:18-25). In Scripture the sexual relationship has a special, almost holy, character to it. Sexual union is symbolic of the spiritual union of Christ and His church (Eph. 5:21-33); pornography separates sexuality from love, and really from human relationships. When sex becomes a spectator activity, a function of mere biology, it is fundamentally destructive to our wholeness and health. For those who believe our wholeness, body, and spirit are made in God's image and that we have an imputed dignity, the degradation and exploitation involved in pornography are the chief evils. It is not the mere arousal of the sexual appetite which defines pornography. Rather, pornography is that which treats human beings obscenely, essentially denying their humanness. A strong defender of pornography, Susan Sontag, admits this split between our personhood and sex: "What pornographic literature does is precisely to drive a wedge between one's existence as a full human being and one's existence as a sexual being."

Release or Entrapment?

We often hear it alleged that pornography is a sort of release for the emotionally-burdened—a nondestructive way to handle pent-up feelings and emotions. But actually pornography is addictive. Despite the claims that pornography is essentially boring and that people will become satiated and it will self-destruct, the evidence is quite to the contrary. There has been, both in our culture as a whole and in the cases of many individuals, a tendency to demand more and more extremes. Malcolm Muggeridge noted this in his volume, *Tread Softly for You Tread on My Jokes*:

> It may be questioned how far it is prudent to subject human beings, as is done today, to ceaseless stimulation. The effect is certainly not to deliver them from obsessive appetites, but rather to keep them in a permanently inflamed condition.

How about the Law?

Law can't create morality or change people's attitudes, so the law ought to stay out of moral questions. That's the contention. But it tragically misses the point.

There are limits to law and government power. There are occasions when restrictive governments impede the creativity and the just rights of persons. Some nations have stifling and oppressive governments that do not permit diversity or dissent. But that is not our problem. Our problem is that our government has forgotten that at the heart of democracy is not only liberty, but restraint.

The law cannot compel morality, but it can teach what it is and it can make immorality more difficult and expensive. The law can shape our attitudes. It can model a nation's highest visions and not its lowest.

What is obscenity? As difficult as it is to develop legal definitions of obscenity, most people do in fact know when a piece of literature or a performance has, as its predominant purpose, a prurient interest—a pandering spirit and a degradation of sexual relationships.

Obscenity is against the law; it is not protected by the First Amendment. The Court has certainly expanded the range of speech permissible under the First Amendment, including often offensive and explicit speech. The Court's eagerness to so broadly protect speech has drawn fire from many quarters who allege neither the founders, the people, nor the preservation of democracy require such lack of restraints. But the course is now well set. As Justice Potter Stewart declared in *Ginzburg vs. U.S.*, "The Constitution protects coarse expression as well as refined, and vulgarity no less than elegance."

The Court has, however, consistently rejected any view that obscenity is protected speech under the First Amendment. "Free speech" has never been absolute. Speech which presents a "clear and present danger" to society such as sedition or threats to immediate disturbance of the peace have never been protected. Nor have libel or slander. In spite of repeated attempts by litigants to urge the Court to hold that the First Amendment protects all speech including obscenity, the Court has refused.

The Court has recognized society's interests in preventing the commercialization of obscenity. Chief Justice Warren Burger, in *Paris Adult Theater I vs. Slaton* (1973), writing for the majority, spoke of the state's "long recognized legitimate interest in regulating the use of obscene material," and the legitimate interests in "stemming the tide of commercialized obscenity." The Court noted some of the public interests as the "quality of life," "total community environment," "tone of commerce," and "public safety." Quoting Earl Warren, the Court declared the "right of the nation and of the states to maintain a decent society."

But What Is Obscene?

Here the courts have substantially limited the kinds of materials which will pass the test. Many offensive materials will not legally be "obscene." On the other hand, a vast array of materials now widely distributed—films, books, magazines—would be obscene under the Court's rules.

The Court has struggled with a definition which does not excessively intrude government into personal life and private rights, but which can, as Burger noted, "stem the tide." In 1973 in *Miller vs. California,* the Court, in a narrow 5-4 decision, developed a three-part test for obscenity. They rejected an earlier test which had required that to be obscene, a work must be "utterly without redeeming social value." That test had proved totally unworkable. So-called experts were always available to declare that some idea, quote, or scene had some "social value." A critic of that rule, writing in the *Christian Science Monitor,* suggested that "by the same logic, it might some day be ruled legal by the Supreme Court to give poison to someone if it is administered within a food high in vitamins or with redeeming, wholesome, nourishing ingredients. Just don't give it to him straight."

The Court in *Miller* established this test:

The basic guidelines for the trier of fact must be: (a) whether the average person, applying contemporary community standards would find the work, taken as a whole, appeals to the prurient interest . . . ; (b) whether the work depicts or describes in a patently offensive way, sexual conduct specifically defined by the applicable state law; and (c) whether the work, taken as a whole, lacks serious literary, artistic, political, or scientific value.

The significance of the new test lies in several areas. First, now "community standards" are relevant and the test of obscenity may vary from San Francisco to Peoria. What is perceived as prurient is in part a function of the community's beliefs. Second, the work is to be judged "taken as a whole." No longer will one quote from Voltaire save an otherwise obscene piece.

It remains clear that mere nudity will not pass the test since the test speaks of "sexual conduct." The Court declared, "We now confine the permissible scope of such regulations to works which depict or describe sexual conduct." The Court went on to describe what would clearly fall within part (b): "Patently offensive representations or descriptions of ultimate sexual acts, normal or perverted, actual or simulated . . . (and) patently offensive representations or descriptions of masturbation, excretory functions, and lewd exhibition of the genitals."

The new rules are not without ambiguity. What is the relevant community for the application of standards? What is patently offensive? What is an "appeal" to prurient interests? But the decision does in theory give the power and the direction to law enforcement units to act against much of the pornography flooding the nation. Convictions can and have been gained in cases where prosecutors properly apply these standards. Larry Flynt and *Hustler* magazine have been convicted in Atlanta. Adult bookstores and porno shops closed down in communities like Salt Lake City and Cincinnati.

If It's Illegal, Why Is It Growing?

Though the Supreme Court's *Miller* decision made prosecution substantially easier, the flood of pornography seems undaunted. There are several reasons for this.

First, these legal remedies are applied only to obscenity and not to the much broader class of literature and media which may be morally offensive. As standards and community beliefs have grown more accepting, the range of materials which meet this test has probably shrunk. But, as noted, much of the pornography sold today would clearly fall within the *Miller* test.

Second, though laws are on the books in virtually every state, few are enforced or applied. Prosecutors seem to lack the interest or the will to pursue the distributors of obscene materials. Some do not enforce the laws because they don't believe in them;

others, because they lack time or sufficient experience. They know that defense lawyers will be well equipped and it will involve extensive trials. The liberal community will not support them.

Third, the public does not demand action. People do not seem to care or to complain when action is not taken.

Fourth, all too often when action *is* taken, arrests made and prosecution commenced, local judges are reluctant to enforce the laws—finding loopholes, declaring some local statute unconstitutional on very shallow grounds, or otherwise discouraging prosecutions.

Fifth, judges apply or the statutes provide only minimal penalties. In many instances, the statutory penalties are minimal. William Stanmeyer noted that the fine for distributing adulterated eggs or selling products that violate noise emission standards is $50,000 per day. If convicted of the sexual exploitation of children, the fine is $10,000! Stanmeyer concludes, "It is at least two-and-one-half times more evil to sell adulterated eggs than it is to show children on videotape committing adultery."

What Should We Do?
Christians have every right to expect that the law will be enforced. We need to encourage law enforcement personnel to prosecute clear instances of the sale of obscene materials. Political leaders must know that we monitor their willingness to act within the law.

To avoid extremes, we need to educate the Christian community about what may be legally barred and what may not. We must avoid the easy tendency to look to the law to halt a broad range of literature which we may find offensive.

In regard to materials which are not legally obscene, but which are still clearly pornographic, we have every right to urge places of business to stop selling such materials. Our efforts ought to begin with our requests to management to remove the offensive materials, explaining why we believe they are not in the best interests of the community and contrary to human values. But if that fails, we ought to be willing to use our economic vote and refuse to deal with such enterprises. Such boycotts, used as a last resort, may be the only effective means to obtain action from some businesses.

7

Criminal Law and the Christian Faith

Answer the following statements true or false:

1. There would be a lot less crime if we had judges   T   F
with stiffer backbones who would order longer prison
terms and less parole.

2. The insanity defense is a crazy idea that ought to   T   F
be forbidden. It's just a lawyer's gimmick to avoid justice.

3. Criminals today have more rights than the victims.   T   F
We ought to eliminate all those technical rules like
reading persons their rights (Miranda warnings) and
excluding evidence just on some technical grounds.

4. Our criminal system, though it has its faults, is the   T   F
best balance between the rights of individuals and the
rights of society.

5. A major cause of crime is the social and economic   T   F
deprivation which is so common in high crime areas.

*   *   *   *   *

Francis Rakowski, a small-time burglar, was recently awarded
$75,000 by a jury after he successfully alleged that one of his
victims had ruined his life by shooting him in the foot. Mrs. Ruth
Clemens, mother of Michael Clemens who shot Rakowski after
discovering him in the act of burglarizing his property, declared:
"He gets rewarded for committing a crime and we get punished."

* * * * *

Jack Henry Abbott stabbed to death Richard Adan on a Manhattan sidewalk. Abbott was a lifelong convict and an author of a best-selling book written during a term in prison. A sympathetic jury found him guilty only of manslaughter, so he'll serve 6 to 10 years. The family of Adan wondered about justice.

* * * * *

Where is the justice? Why do the criminals have all the rights? There is a widespread feeling that the criminal justice system has collapsed and justice is no longer either "swift" or "sure."

Many feel it has all become a clever lawyer's game that has little to do with truth or justice. Paul Montoya, Chief of Detectives in Denver, observed, "We don't have a criminal justice system. . . . This is a lawyer's world . . . the whole judicial system revolves around what lawyers want to do." The endless delays, plea bargaining, exclusion of reliable evidence, and defendants beating the system with technical rules of law are perceived as the machinations of a legal system that has lost its commitment to truth.

And what about the victims? Who helps them? They are the wounded, the intimidated, the assaulted. The system marshals public defenders, constitutional experts, courts, police investigators, court reporters, and the whole array of the state arise to both prosecute and defend the perpetrator. Who cares for the victim?

These concerns are not merely those of frightened rednecks. Chief Justice Warren Burger warned the American Bar Association that we are "fast approaching the status of an impotent society."

The U.S. has the highest crime rate in the Western world. Each year 1 person in 100 will be robbed and 1 in 10 households will have a burglary or an attempted burglary. Statistics show that there is:

- one murder every 23 minutes
- one rape every 6 minutes
- one burglary every 8 seconds
- one violent crime every 24 seconds

Crimes by youth constitute one of the most frightening phenomena. One study showed that nearly half of all those arrested for felonies were under the age of 18, a rate that tripled between 1960 and 1975. Yet only 3 to 7 percent of those arrested are ever punished in any form.

It is no wonder "law and order" is a frequent cry. And as if the traditional crimes were not enough, there is also the enormous growth in organized crime, the explosion of illegal drugs, and the rise of white-collar crime. If we add tax evasion, corporate crime, and the unreported theft by employees from their employers, then it is clear that crime is as theologian L. Harold DeWolf noted in 1975, "a struggle with the very existence of our democratic republic."

Crime Doesn't Pay

Don't you believe it. It pays. The odds are low that if you commit a crime you will ever be punished. Fewer than 25 percent of index crimes (murder, rape, robbery, burglary, aggravated assault, larceny-theft, and motor vehicle theft) ever even lead to an arrest. Of those arrested, only 38 percent are found guilty. Only 14 percent of burglaries lead to any arrest. One study concluded less than 3½ percent of felonies resulted in any person serving jail or prison time.

Who's at Fault?

Why do we lack the will or the resources to restrain crime? Whose fault is this mess? Many blame the legal system. They believe that under the guise of rights and reform, our system has stripped police powers, emphasized the rights of the accused, and routinely permitted dangerous persons to be released on bail pending trial or has released dangerous persons into the community on parole.

There are, to be sure, tragic stories. In 1979 a 51-year-old artist was fatally beaten in Washington, D.C. Two of the men charged were free on bail, one of them in connection with rape charges. And the rape charge had been made when he was on probation from an earlier assault. In a Washington, D.C. study,

26 percent of all felonies were committed by persons out on some form of conditional release.

Many people blame the collapse of our primary social institutions and values. In *The Public Interest,* James Q. Wilson says that our philosophy which "recognizes no limits," "emphasizes rights," and "which implies a preference for . . . self-expression over self-restraint" is at the core of our dilemma. He acknowledges the role of urban flight by the middle class, diminishing opportunities for urban young, "the corrosive effects of . . . racism," and the availability of guns, but believes these are often but consequences of the "ethos of self-expression" which dominates our culture. Wilson concludes:

> The demise of Victorian morality, the inability of the state to recreate the morality, and the growth in personal freedom and social prosperity, have combined to produce an individualistic ethos that both encourages crime and shapes the kind of policies we are prepared to use to combat it. . . . The factors that most directly influence crime—family structure, moral development, the level of personal freedom—are the very things we cannot easily change.

Others prefer to focus on the elements Wilson sees as secondary. They look to social and economic factors such as the predilection to violence in our society, materialism, racism, unemployment, and despair. These people point out that certain groups tend to have little identity with the "establishment." Law and order are merely code words for those in power. The police are perceived as enemies.

So what do we do? Conservatives often speak out for tougher laws, more police, more prisons, speedier trials, capital punishment, perhaps abolishing the insanity defense. Liberals urge an emphasis on social and economic factors in crime, alternatives to prisons, more controls on police misconduct, counseling and diversion from the judicial system, and jobs programs. Liberals often urge gun control.

The reality is few of us know much about the criminal justice system. We are happy to let others take care of it. We don't want to get involved.

For most of us, crime and criminals seem strictly like a "black hats" and "white hats" situation. Crime involves "them"—criminals, crooks, junkies, and riffraff. On the other side are the police and the good folks. We are usually content to convict the guilty and lock them up. We are blind to the complexities of the system and to the injustices which often occur. We are unaware of the difficult tasks which both police and public defenders have.

A Christian Perspective

There is no specifically Christian view of our criminal justice system. Scripture does not give much counsel about the exclusionary rule or the Miranda warnings. There is, however, a recurring theme of the duty of the believing community to minister to prisoners. Jesus read from Isaiah 61:1 when He announced His Messiahship. The passage speaks of a calling to "proclaim liberty to the captives." Jesus offered forgiveness to those being crucified with Him and spoke of those who visited prisoners as visiting Him. The church has always recognized a calling to minister to prisoners, and Christians have played significant roles in many reform efforts. Clearly the church cannot ignore persons merely because they have been convicted of crimes. But beyond this pastoral concern, there are some emphases which give to Christians a perspective on these issues.

First, our faith teaches us the reality of sin. Sin is endemic, a product of our alienation from God, and stands under God's judgment. This conviction leads to a concept of responsibility for one's acts. While by no means denying the environmental factors in creating conditions which may give rise to criminal conduct, Christians maintain a strong sense of responsibility of a person for his acts.

That one is accountable for one's behavior may appear too obvious to point out, yet some people see crime as simply a product of environment. The sociologist Durkheim even goes so far as to speak of the "normality of crime." This view sees crime as simply a sociological category, devoid of moral substance. Others believe that criminals are simply "sick" and therefore only in need of "treatment." Some schools of psychology and psychiatry are inclined to speak this way.

The Christian's belief in the reality of sin bars any rigid categorizing of "criminals." Sin is universal. This does not require a winking at crime, but it will preclude any idea that criminals are essentially different from other persons. Criminals cannot be ignored, labeled, denied jobs, shunned, and denied the redemptive relationships which the church is to offer the world.

Second, as believers we should also have a special regard for justice. Justice will not necessarily make us "tough" on crime. We must consider the inequities in our criminal justice system. When police violate the rights of persons, when witnesses lie, when prosecutors exceed their authority—then justice will speak out for those arrested.

We should surely be disturbed when corporate crimes and tax evasion by prominent political and social figures are treated with a slap on the wrist, while theft by a young person, usually without significant legal representation, leads to a prison term. Then Solicitor-General of the United States, Simon Sobeloff, reported two cases which came before the same judge. In one case, a bank cashier stole enormous sums of money and hid the crimes for years. When finally convicted, the defendant received a suspended sentence. In the other case, an 18-month prison term was given to a young boy for selling song sheets without obtaining permission of the copyright owners. As Sobeloff declared, "Such fantastic vagaries tear down the mightiest sanction of the law—respect for the courts."

We should be deeply concerned when the ability to afford legal counsel seems determinative of one's success at insuring rights, or whenever economic means affect rights to effective counsel or seem to be determinative of the type and length of sentences. We cannot be blind to the impact of race, for example, on the nature of judicial penalties.

Third, Christians should see judgment and punishment as also having the intention of leading persons to repentance. The discipline of the state is to punish evil, but God's intention is that such discipline should awaken conscience and invite one to a new life. This does not mean that Christians should either be "soft" or "hard" on issues of punishment. Instead, we should be sensitive to whether that punishment is the one which best serves justice and the hope for repentance.

Fourth, biblical principles of reconciliation and concern for those who suffer should give us a special sensitivity to the needs of victims. We must recognize the emotional and physical trauma of many victims and seek to be healing agents. Christians believe in what appears to be humanly impossible—that God can reconcile the perpetrator and the victim. God wills repentance, restitution, and forgiveness.

Interest in victims has increased significantly in recent years. Several states such as Wisconsin have adopted a "victim's bill of rights." Thirty-eight states have some type of compensation programs for crime victims. These programs assist in covering out-of-pocket losses to innocent victims of crimes.

Such innovations seem appropriate and worthy of support, though they naturally cannot offer the full emotional and spiritual help that victims often need, nor the impetus to reconciliation which lies at the core of the human situation. Some interesting models are being tested where victims and offenders are brought together to provide the occasion for apology, forgiveness, restitution, and reconciliation. The Victim-Offender Reconciliation Project in Elkhart, Indiana, administered largely by Mennonite members of that community, has sought to implement these principles.

The issues in the criminal field are enormously complex. Two issues that have generated strong opinion and public action are the appropriateness of the "exclusionary rule" and the insanity defense. A brief look at these two issues may help us understand the complexity of such questions.

The Exclusionary Rule

A woman who lived alone was accosted in her bedroom at night, robbed, and raped at knife point. In the dim light she noticed the defendant's leather boots and knife. As soon as he left, she phoned police who found boot tracks in the area and traced them to the defendant's home. After knocking and entering, the police observed the defendant with his boots on. He was questioned and told to go outside and place his boots in the tracks. The boots were confiscated and he was taken before a magistrate. The house was then searched and the knife was found. The defendant was convicted.

The conviction was overturned by a court which held the arrest and search were illegal (*Woods vs. State,* Texas 1971).

Incidents such as this, repeated in various forms in courts almost daily, have created an outcry from both the public and law enforcement personnel concerning the "rights" of defendants which create injustices. All too often these "rights" have little to do with whether the defendant is actually guilty.

Have we overdone the protection of criminal defendants? Or is it a central aspect of our civil liberties against irresponsible state power?

Much of the criticism has been directed to the Supreme Court, which during the "Warren" years, expanded the procedural protections afforded to those charged with crimes. The Court's most well-known protection was the *Miranda* decision, requiring that those arrested be "read their rights." The Court based these rulings on the Constitution protections of due process, equal protection, right to a jury trial, right to confront witnesses, and prohibition against illegal searches and seizures.

The Fourth Amendment provides for the "right of the people to be secure . . . against unreasonable searches and seizures" and requires that warrants authorizing a reasonable search must be specific and based on "probable cause." Based on that protection, the Supreme Court in *Mapp vs. Ohio* (1961) adopted what has become perhaps the most controversial of these protections— the exclusionary rule. In *Mapp,* the Supreme Court reversed a conviction based on evidence that had been seized without a proper search warrant. The Court declared that if illegally seized evidence, such as papers and things, could be used as evidence in a criminal prosecution, the protections of the Fourth Amendment would be of "no value" and "might as well be stricken from the Constitution."

Though noting that some guilty persons may go free as a result, the Court declared that "nothing can destroy a government more quickly than its failure to observe its own laws." Thus, the Court established a rule that the prosecution may not use any evidence which is the result of an illegal search or seizure.

On the surface, the rule does not seem all that surprising. In fact, however, the rule has been vigorously attacked as not only a total failure in achieving the goals set forth by Brennan, but as contributing to manifest injustice. Dallin Oaks, Justice on the Utah Supreme Court, conducted a study and concluded, "As a device for deterring illegal searches and seizures by the police, the exclusionary rule is a failure." Justice Warren Burger, in a dissenting opinion, summarized the essential criticisms of the rule:

> The costs of . . . the exclusionary rule . . . are well known: (1) The focus of the trial [is] diverted from the ultimate question of guilt or innocence . . . (2) the physical evidence sought to be excluded is typically reliable and often the most probative information . . . (3) the rule often frees the guilty . . . (4) the rule is contrary to the idea of proportionality that is essential to the concept of justice . . . (5) it may well have the effect of generating disrespect for the law.

One problem is that this rule is not clear about what searches and seizures are illegal. The courts have been wrestling with borderline cases for two decades. The uncertainty of the rule is illustrated by two cases discussed in an article by U.S. Attorney General designate Ed Meese. A California case and a New York case both involved police officers who stopped a car, smelled marijuana, ordered the passengers out of the car, and discovered marijuana in the passenger compartment. As the officers made a legal arrest, they discovered further drugs during the frisk searches. The cases found their way to the Supreme Court. Of the nine justices, three held both searches legal, three held both illegal, and three found one legal and the other not. And the search found legal by the Supreme Court had earlier been found illegal by a state court, and the search found illegal had been held legal by that state's Supreme Court. As Meese notes, "By the time it was over, 14 justices in three jurisdictions had ruled on the case. And interestingly enough, they came out . . . 7 to 7. Now, that may be good enough for Solomon, but it's not much help to the police officer at 2 A.M."

Various alternatives have been suggested, including police disciplinary procedures for violating officers perhaps conducted by an independent review board, a statutory right to bring civil suits against police for violations, and a limited use of the exclusionary rule in cases of serious felonies such as murder, treason, rape, etc. What is essential to much of the criticism is that the wrong-doers, the police, are not really the ones punished. In fact, no one is.

Current attempts to modify the rule focus on the creation of a "good faith" exemption. The Attorney General's Task Force on Violent Crime recommended that the rule be applied only in those cases in which a judge finds that the police officer acted in "bad faith," knowing that the search was in violation of the law. Legislation advocating this approach has been introduced in Congress.

Critics fear adoption of such a rule would discourage careful attention to rights by police. Ignorance would become an excuse. It would increase, they fear, the number of illegal searches and set back the effort to compel police to respect rights of privacy.

A Word of Caution

We must remember that the protections provided by the Constitution and applied by the courts do reflect some central commitments in our society. The presumptions of innocence and rights of those charged are intended to insure that the greatest protections are afforded persons from improper actions by the government. The founders of our nation had had enough of the indiscretion of officials who enforced laws in an arbitrary and capricious manner. They constructed a legal system which recognized that some guilty persons would indeed go free as part of the assurance of individual liberty and that the innocent would have minimal risk of conviction. Our commitment is indeed that it is better that some guilty go free than that the innocent be convicted or that fundamental rights of the people be infringed.

Undoubtedly changes are appropriate from time to time in any system and we should not hesitate to correct abuses. However, a familiarity with the lack of such protections in so many parts of the world should help us appreciate the protections afforded in our system. It ought to be with great caution that we diminish individual rights merely to assure easier convictions or give the police special powers. We can too easily forget that the Constitution was largely intended as a limit on the powers of the government. The colonists experienced oppressive government and they fully intended to limit the tools at the state's disposal. The reality of evil in the world would warrant the maintenance of such a protection.

The Insanity Plea: A Rule Gone Awry?

My actions on March 30, 1981 have given special meaning to my life and no amount of imprisonment or hospitalization can tarnish my historical deed. . . . I . . . committed the ultimate crime in hopes of winning the heart of a girl. It was an unprecedented demonstration of love. But does the American public appreciate what I've done?

So wrote John Hinckley to the *New York Times* two weeks after a Washington, D.C. jury had found him not guilty by reason of insanity in the assassination attempt on President Ronald Reagan.

Americans not only didn't appreciate Hinckley's act, they didn't like the jury's either. The outcry was immediate. Over 50 bills were introduced in Congress to abolish or substantially modify the insanity plea. Several states, including Illinois and Idaho, responded promptly by abolishing the plea and substituting a "guilty but insane" plea.

The jury's problem was a common one. The acts of Hinckley seemed absurd. People would commonly say he was "crazy." Could anyone who does such a thing possibly be sane? Could it be that the more absurd and heinous the offense, the more likely one is to get off?

The Hinckley case was not alone. On September 24, 1978 California Angels' baseball player Lyman Bostock was gunned down by Leonard Smith, former husband of a woman Bostock was visiting. In November 1979, after hearing psychiatrists tell of Smith's difficult life, a jury found Leonard Smith not guilty by reason of insanity. On June 21, 1980 Leonard Smith walked out of a state hospital a free man, only seven months after a jury said he was insane. As one commentator concluded, "In effect, the criminal justice system told Leonard Smith he could have one almost-free murder to make up for his sad life."

Though the insanity defense is rarely successful, critics have been increasingly vocal. President Nixon declared the insanity defense an "unconscionable abuse." The American Medical Association Board of Trustees in November 1983 recommended the abolition of the plea except in sentencing considerations. Board Chairman John Coury, Jr., explained, "It seems the insanity defense is being used to escape responsibility for just about any crime."

The Origin of the Concept

The notion that persons who are not in control of their behavior should not be liable for their acts is an ancient one. The Babylonian Talmud exempted "a deaf-mute, an idiot, and a minor" from liability for injuries they caused others. Aristotle held that persons were responsible only if they had knowledge of their acts and freedom to choose. Early English law provided not for acquittal, but mitigation of punishment or pardons for "madmen" who were seen as akin to a "wild beast."

Modern law begins with a case which created the same sort of uproar as Hinckley's. The 1843 case involved Daniel M'Naghten, who believed that the British Prime Minister Sir Robert Peel and others were conspiring against him. On January 20, 1843 M'Naghten shot and killed Edward Drummond, Peel's secretary, believing him to be Peel. At his trial, nine medical witnesses testified he was insane, and the jury found him not guilty on the grounds of insanity.

Both Houses of Parliament immediately debated the insanity defense and forwarded to 15 judges a series of questions. Their answers now constitute the famous "M'Naghten" test of insanity, sometimes referred to as the "right/wrong" test. Under this test, which became the predominant standard in America, the accused is not criminally responsible if a mental disease, at the time, prevented him from knowing the nature and quality of the act or that it was wrong.

Some states have broadened the test by adding the "irresistible impulse" test, which also exempts persons where a disease of the mind prevents them from controlling their conduct. Under M'Naghten, *knowledge* is the key, but the "irresistible impulse" test adds an element of loss of *capacity*.

Several states have adopted other versions which have been seen as more "liberal" and which give less emphasis to knowledge of "right and wrong." The Durham Rule focuses on acts which are the "product of mental disease or defect" (product test). The Model Penal Code offers still another version, exempting persons who "lack substantial capacity either to appreciate the wrongfulness of his conduct or to conform his conduct to the requirements of law."

Criticisms

None of these formulas has escaped criticism. No matter what the test, many note that trials often become a "battle of experts" with psychiatrists hired by both sides offering "expert testimony" that is totally contradictory.

Nor do these formulas seem to help the jury make appropriate legal decisions. Few of those now found not guilty really qualify under the M'Naghten test, or even under more liberal versions.

These tests do not help society determine what ought to happen on an acquittal. Few of the jurors in the Leonard Smith trial probably had any notion he could be on the streets in 14 months. But what should happen if a person is acquitted on grounds of insanity and then the very profession which argued he was insane, later finds him no longer insane? Who ought to decide? Is a judgment of insane almost a life sentence—till cured?

Many also criticize the fact that in most states, once the defense raises the insanity plea, it is the state's task to prove the defendant is sane, and it must prove this beyond a reasonable doubt.

The Philosophic Premise of the Defense

Perhaps few have thought of the insanity defense as raising fundamental questions about human nature. Yet a basic principle in the insanity defense is the concept of freedom of choice and responsibility. The entire criminal law is built on the belief that persons are responsible for their acts—that they are free to choose and are subject to criminal punishment when they choose to act against the law. Such a notion is fully compatible with and reinforced by Christian convictions about sin, guilt, and accountability. The insanity defense is built upon this concept. Setting aside the abuses, its principle is that when persons do not know what they are doing or do not know that what they are doing is wrong, then they are not responsible. Guilt is a function of knowledge and will. Our whole law recognizes this. We do not punish first-degree murder the same as involuntary manslaughter or a total accident. Guilt assumes more than that one did the act, but that one has done "wrong." "To him that knoweth to do good and doeth it not, to him it is sin" (James 4:17). It is the guilty mind that rests at the base of the wrongfulness. In criminal law, this concept is also prominent. To be guilty of a crime, one must have the requisite *mens rea*—a legal term for bad intent, bad will—or there is no crime. Though the insanity defense may go beyond mere *mens rea* questions, its philosophic base is the same.

Contrasting Criticism
Criticisms of the insanity defense have come from two quite disparate sources and represent two contrasting philosophic viewpoints.

On the one hand are the critics who suggest that the concepts of human freedom and responsibility are myths and therefore distinguishing moral culpability is an illusion. Since the insanity defense is rooted in such distinctions, it ought to be abolished. The focus should be solely on the conduct, not on the state of mind and freedom of choice. For many the notions of guilt, blame, free will, and responsibility need to be replaced with more sociological categories. R.J. Gerber, writing in the *American Journal of Jurisprudence,* rightly refers to such viewpoints as a *"Clockwork Orange* scenario. . . . A degrading picture of human responsibility [which] will never appeal to more than mad academics."

The other view on the insanity defense comes from those willing to accept the notion of responsibility. They believe the insanity defense has become abused, actually avoiding the imposition of responsibility. They are concerned with the dominance of psychiatrists usurping the juries' roles. They fear that, as William J. Winslade suggested in *The Insanity Plea,* jurors unfamiliar with the "vagueness and imprecision" of the assumptions of psychiatrists may well take them as "far more precise and scientifically accurate than they in fact are."

Alternatives

Two basic alternatives have been suggested. One focuses on the abolition of the insanity defense. The Attorney General's Task Force on Violent Crime recommended such and urged its replacement by a plea of "guilty but insane." This plea would require an admission of guilt and the mental illness would become a factor in the treatment or sentencing.

The second alternative is to restrict the rules under which the defense may be raised. Some jurisdictions have shifted the burden of proof, requiring the defendant to show that he is insane. Other reforms have focused on more judicial review of medical profession decisions regarding the eligibility for release from confinement of one who had been hospitalized following a successful insanity plea. Others have suggested attempts to create a neutral expert panel rather than rely on the "battle of the experts."

Since the insanity plea goes to the heart of our convictions about human responsibility, and since assessing another person's state of mind is obviously very difficult, the issue is not likely to disappear. While abuses may well need correction, the basic concept is founded on principles of human nature fully compatible with Christian thought.

8

Holy
Disobedience

Item: The lights went on and the television cameras began to whir. On the platform of the Faith Baptist Church in Louisville, Nebraska was Reverend Everett Sileven. Off to the side were a number of sheriff's deputies. In the front row were little children. The cameras watched their faces as the sheriff's deputies walked up to Reverend Sileven, took him into custody, and took him to the Cass County jail to serve a term for contempt of court. Sileven had refused to comply with a court order barring operation of a church private school unless it met state standards for teachers. A padlock was placed on the door of the school.

Item: "We turned the rotunda into a sanctuary," declared the Sojourners, referring to their "Witness for Peace" demonstration at the Capitol on Pentecost Sunday 1983. Jim Wallis, Sojourners' leader and coordinator of the protest, said, "We were arrested for praying for peace." He wrote a letter to supporters: "I'm writing this letter from jail. . . . This is a taste of things to come."

Item: A *National Coalition of Unregistered Churches* has formed to oppose government regulation and aid resisters.

Item: Gary Bergel of Intercessors for America, complaining of the application of social security laws to churches, declared: "If our forefathers resisted a tax on *tea,* what would they do with this?"

Item: The Moral Majority Report of September 21, 1981 suggested the possibility of withholding taxes over the abortion issue if the Human Life Amendment didn't pass. A group in southern Illinois, the Army of God, went a step further and kidnapped the operators of a local abortion clinic. Judge Randy Heckman, confronted with a request to approve an abortion for a minor, declined to do so in spite of the fact that legal precedents would seem to have required such consent. Declared Heckman: "When a judge is faced with the option of doing that which is ultimately just versus that which is morally legal, he ought to choose the just—and be willing to suffer, if need be, the consequences of doing so."

What is going on? Are people taking the law into their own hands or are we seeing a recovery of obedience to God? Are we watching saints or criminals, martyrs or demagogues? Whatever it is, it seems to be growing.

A relatively recent phenomenon is the advocacy of civil disobedience by the more conservative elements in the Christian community. Precisely those elements which attacked civil disobedience in the civil rights movement of the 1960s and the Vietnam War protests of the 1970s are now dusting off the doctrine for their own use. Francis Schaeffer in *The Christian Manifesto* warns against an idolatry of the state and demands that Christians recognize their potential duty to resist evil government. "If there is no place for civil disobedience, then the government has been made autonomous, and as such, it has been put in the place of the Living God." He suggests that Christians might at some point refuse to pay a portion of taxes which support abortion. "It's time for Christians and others who do not accept the narrow and bigoted humanist views rightfully to use the appropriate forms of protest."

Why now? What has changed the minds of those who earlier spoke of a duty to obey government and warned of lawlessness and arrogance? The increased tensions between the values of government and the values of religious persons introduce more and more occasions where the policies of the government run counter to the beliefs and morals of active minorities in communities. Combine these factors with an increased sense of government interference, a heightened involvement in public issues by Christians, and visible leaders attacking government institutions such as the courts and you have the ingredients for holy disobedience.

Such acts are, of course, illegal. By definition, acts of civil disobedience cannot be condoned by the legal system. The law at times seeks to make provisions for certain acts based on convictions of conscience. Statutes, for example, permit exemption from military service. The "conscience clause" in federal labor law permits exemption on religious grounds from membership in labor unions. Constitutional protection of free exercise of religion also requires that any governmental interference with a sincerely held religious belief be based on a compelling government interest and that the intrusion be as minimal as possible.

But civil disobedience is something else. It is a deliberate violation of the law normally based on a personal conviction that the law is immoral—that a "higher law" or an inner duty to conscience requires one to say no to government.

In addition to the claim of conscience, other oft-cited characteristics of civil disobedience are the public or open character of the act, the use of nonviolent means, and the willingness to accept the punishment for the violation. In this sense, civilly disobedient acts are not a total rejection of the law, nor are they revolutionary. The actor accepts the authority of the state and does not hide his acts.

Two Kinds of Civil Disobedience

There are two types of civil disobedience. First is what some call "conscientious disobedience." This involves situations where an individual, for reasons of conscience, refuses to perform some required government act (bowing to an idol, taking up weapons, registering a school), or persists in performing some prohibited act (preaching, counseling draft resistance, operating an un-licensed school). The person does not object to the government's authority in general, nor necessarily even oppose the particular law itself. The individual merely insists that for reasons of conscience, he or she cannot obey. These acts do not normally threaten the government; they are almost totally passive. Examples include refusal to participate in war, refusal of Christians to worship idols (Shadrach, Meshach, and Abed-nego). This type of civil disobedience does not emphasize any mission to change government or make it Christian.

The second and more common type of civil disobedience poses a greater threat to an orderly society. Here the acts of civil disobedience take on an increasingly public and political character. They are intended to pressure the government, to morally embarrass the authorities, or to educate the public. The purpose for this kind of civil disobedience is to change the law. Examples are the civil rights and Vietnam War protests. Christians who are involved in this type of civil disobedience see a biblical responsibility to develop a just government.

Some people also distinguish between *direct* and *indirect* civil disobedience. In *direct* civil disobedience, the law disobeyed is the law objected to, for example compulsory military service, laws requiring registration of church schools, or laws prohibiting public evangelism in the Soviet Union. In *indirect* civil disobedience, the law actually violated is not the law objected to. For example, a sit-in in a restaurant that results in an arrest for trespassing is not an objection to the trespass laws, but an objection to a larger policy—discrimination.

Conscience

Central to the philosophy and practice of civil disobedience throughout history has been the notion of the importance of conscience. The Scriptures speak powerfully about the spirit witnessing to our conscience. Writers have frequently suggested that there is a public interest in encouraging such faithfulness to the inner voice. As Abraham Kuyper, Calvinist theologian, noted: "A nation consisting of citizens whose consciences are bruised is itself broken in its national strength." Another suggested that to resist conscience was to waste the "spiritual capital" of a society. Not all have agreed. Roger Williams, who insisted on the right of personal concience, was banished in 1635 for advocating such a right and was tried by a general court of the Massachusetts colony.

Such claims of conscience may seem powerful and compelling to the actor. As Daniel Berrigan, a prominent and radical activist in civil disobedience connected with the Vietnam War who served a prison term declared, "I could not *not* break the law and remain human . . . if we kept forever on this side of the line, we would die within." The story is told that when Ralph Waldo Emerson visited Thoreau, who was in jail for refusing to pay taxes he believed aided a war effort to advance slavery, Emerson reportedly asked, "What are you doing in there?" to which Thoreau responded: "What are *you* doing out *there?*"

But is conscience a sufficient guide? Scripture indicates that we should not solely trust in our own personal judgment because conscience may be "seared" (1 Tim. 4:2). Conscience may be insensitive and need a prophetic reminder. The Word of God is to inform our conscience.

As central as conscience may be, neither the law, the community, nor Christians are bound to give credence or protection to one's personal claim of "conscience." Conscience may too easily be shaped by self-delusion, trained to support one's private views, and excuse one's duty and responsibility to others. Conscience too is subject to sin.

There is in fact a special danger for the religiously motivated, civilly disobedient. Such persons often become totally inflexible, identifying their personal rights and beliefs with God. They demand, in God's name, full surrender from all others. They become crusaders—blind to counsel and reason. Every issue is a "holy crusade."

We often hear about people who insist that God told them to do some terrible thing. Recently a man charged with killing his children insisted he was doing what God told him. Civil disobedience advocate, Bedeau, declared: "It does not follow from the fact that a man cannot do more than whatever he thinks he ought to do, that he ought to do whatever he thinks he ought to do." As Frank Johnson, writing in the *University of Florida Law Review,* observed: "The man who chooses on grounds of conscience may be a saint or a madman." Truman Nelson put it more directly: "One may be an individual like John Bunyan and sit in jail for acting against the state, and write *Pilgrim's Progress.* Or, like Hitler, and write *Mein Kampf.*"

Historical Antecedents

General William Booth, the founder of the Salvation Army, declared: "No great cause ever achieved a triumph before it furnished a certain quota to the prison population." Civil disobedience is as old as government and the philosophic problems of civil disobedience are by no means new. History is full of martyrs and heroes who stood against the tide. Some of them were successful, but more often they were ridiculed, exiled, imprisoned, or killed. Gary North, editor of *The Theology of Christian Resistance,* observed that "ultimately, the history of Western civilization is the history of Christians' struggles against unlawful state power."

Christians have often said no! The early Hutterites refused taxes for the hangman's noose. John Bunyan refused to buy a license to preach. When Polycarp was arrested in A.D. 156, he refused to declare "Caesar is Lord" and was burned at the stake. Several Quakers were hanged under laws in Massachusetts in the 1650s barring Quakers from trying to hold a meeting for worship. Those not hanged were often beaten, branded, or had their ears cropped.

Theologians have given considerable attention to the duties of Christians in regard to law. St. Augustine saw civil authority as derived from God and therefore within God's plan. He, nevertheless, indicated that when law was in violation of God's law, we must refuse to obey the law. Augustine distinguished between the duty to be *submissive* to government and the duty to *obey* the law. While we have a duty to *submit* to authority, that duty does not extend to *obeying* all the authority's laws. If we must disobey the law, we still submit to the authority, acknowledge the authority's dominion, accept the punishment, and do not seek to overturn it.

It was Thomas Aquinas, however, who spelled this out in more detail. In his *Treatise on Law,* Aquinas said:

Laws framed by man are either just or unjust. If they are just they have the power of binding in conscience from the eternal law from which they are derived. . . . On the other hand, laws must be unjust in two ways. First by being contrary to human good . . . the like are acts of violence rather than laws because as Augustine says: "A law that is not just seems to be no law at all." Therefore such laws do not bind the conscience.

Secondly, laws may be unjust through being opposed to the divine good. Such are the laws of tyrants inducing to idolatry or to anything contrary to the divine law; the laws of this kind must in no way be observed.

Apple Pie and Civil Disobedience

Civil disobedience is as American as apple pie, for our nation was born in an act of civil disobedience, the Revolution. We celebrate events like the Boston Tea Party, sing songs about John Brown, and praise the abolitionists and their illegal Underground Railroad. In 1964, Adlai Stevenson declared: "Even a jail sentence is no longer a dishonor, but a proud achievement. Perhaps we are destined to see in this law-loving land people running for office not on their stainless records, but on their prison records." The civil rights struggle has given civil disobedience a prominent place in our lives. Beginning with the abolitionist movement through the present day, the securing of civil rights has been a history of civil disobedience. Theodore Parker, the abolitionist clergyman, freely appealed for civil disobedience in the light of a higher law:

What shall we do . . . in regard to this present war? We can refuse to take any part in it; we can encourage others to do the same. . . . We are a rebellious nation; our whole history is treason; our blood was tainted before we were born . . . though all the governors of the world bid us commit treason against man, and set the example, let us never submit. Let God only be the master to control our consciences.

The Fugitive Slave Act of 1850 stimulated further civil disobedience. The Underground Railroad expanded with as many as 2,000 fugitives a year during the 1850s reaching Canada. Religious leaders were substantially involved in such efforts.

Henry David Thoreau became an early saint for followers of civil disobedience. His famous essay, "On the Duty of Civil Disobedience," insisted on the right to disobey unjust laws since one dare not resign one's conscience to the legislator. He warned, "The law will never make men free; it is men who have got to make the law free. They are the lovers of law and order, who observe the law when the government breaks it."

Martin Luther King, Jr., inspired by Thoreau and Gandhi, spoke similarly in his "Letter from a Birmingham Jail," written in April 1963. King spoke of a "moral responsibility to disobey unjust laws," citing St. Augustine's claim that "an unjust law is no law at all." Following Gandhi, he insisted that unjust laws must be disobeyed, but must be done so "openly, lovingly, and with a willingness to accept the penalty" so as to "arouse the conscience of the community over injustice" and therefore express "the highest respect for law."

What are Christians to make of all this? When is the law so offensive to the law of God, our sense of right and wrong, and the demands of conscience that we must disobey it or seek rebellion? What does Scripture suggest? Is passive refusal to obey the government permissible? What about active resistance? Political pressure?

Advocates of civil disobedience justify their acts on several grounds. Most speak of the duty to a "higher law" which often requires one to disobey a "lower law." Many suggest that civil disobedience, by refusing to follow *unjust* law, actually shows greater respect for law than mere passive obedience. Law must be called to justice. Others have spoken of our duty to resist evil wherever it is manifest. Government evil is not immune.

More pragmatically inclined defenders insist that only by such acts of courage will society be forced to face its injustices. Where would our society be if it weren't for those who resisted British taxation, fought slavery, refused intimidation by "state" churches in the colonial period, insisted on the vote for women, and fought for civil rights for minorities?

But many have warned of the disintegration of authority once every man has the moral right to disobey the law. If only those who believe it is "right" are bound morally by it, then it can hardly be law. It will lose its authority. Every man will become his own law.

Others warn that once we grant a moral right to disobey law, how can we, as one author put it, "build a fence around it"? How can we deny to all others a right we claim for ourselves? If one may disobey a law for a good purpose, why can't another disobey it for that person's sense of what is "good"? Don't we have a duty to each other to conduct our political and legal affairs without resorting to power tactics? Especially in a democracy where the means of social and political changes are numerous—where we can vote, petition, and advocate—shouldn't we bind ourselves to the decisions that come out of that process? Don't we have a *moral* duty to obey the law?

Biblical Principles

Any biblical thinking about civil disobedience must begin with the central biblical declaration of the sovereignty of God. Either Jehovah is God or Caesar is. Until we settle that question, the issue of civil disobedience never even emerges.

A second biblical principle is the legitimacy of government. Romans 13 makes it clear that government is an institution ordained by God to restrain evil and support good. This legitimacy of government does not extend only to Christian governments. Paul's letter to the Romans was written in a time of a most oppressive government—one that persecuted Christians, one that was linked to a religious cult, the worship of the emperor. It was idolatrous. Nevertheless, it was an instrument of God.

A third biblical principle is the teaching about submission to authority. This submission includes not only our submission to God, but submission to government, servants to masters, children to parents, and submission to the church. There is no radical notion of a full-orbed individualism in Scripture. Instead, the Bible has more to say about duties. Concepts of submission, of course, can easily become perverted. They can become tools of oppression, doctrines that seek to baptize the existing order, theologies which sustain practices of discrimination, slavery, and other acts repeatedly condemned by Scripture.

Fourth is the biblical posture much cited in many civil disobedience movements, the rejection of violence. Contemporary civil disobedience movements as well as Anabaptists for several centuries have highlighted the nonviolent, the nonresistant components of the New Testament (citing the refusal to take up the sword, the acceptance of death, etc.). Such a perspective may be easily overdone. In the Old Testament, righteousness is demonstrated not only by suffering servants, but also by the slaying of false prophets at Mount Carmel; in the New Testament, particularly in the Book of Revelation, battles for righteousness are frequently mentioned.

A final biblical motif is that Christians are a unique and peculiar people. Hebrews 11:13 describes us as pilgrims and strangers on the earth, and Ephesians has images of an alternative citizenship (2:19). In Ephesians 5:6-17 there is the clear concept parallel to the light of the world image in the Gospels, that the people of God know a new reality. We exist as possessors of unique truth in a world structured with lies and illusions. In the world of idolatry, the believer stands in sharp contrast. The believer will at times confound or enrage the high priest of man's secular idolatrous allegiances. The believer contends with principalities and powers. The believer thus stands against the "lie" which is at the foundation of this world.

Specific Biblical Teachings

The examination of the appropriateness and scope of civil disobedience, however, frequently is debated not in terms of these general biblical principles but some specific teachings.

Foremost in the debate has been the significance of Romans 13 with its counsel to obey the civil authorities. Paul commands submission to the government because the authority is ordained of God (v. 1), because resistance to government is ultimately resistance to God (v. 2), because government opposes evil (v. 4), and because our conscience tells us to be subject (v. 5). The text suggests ways in which that obedience is shown, such as taxes, tribute, fear, and honor. But questions still remain: What is lawful authority? What "powers" ought to be obeyed?

The basic teaching is repeated again in Titus 3:1: "Put them in mind to be subject to principalities and powers, to obey magistrates, to be ready to every good work." This passage is often linked to similar teachings in 1 Peter 2:13-17. Here Peter also advises believers to obey the government because it is ordained by God and thus obeying the government is obeying God (v. 13), it is the will of God (v. 15), and it is a good testimony to the unsaved.

These passages form the basis of evangelicals' arguments against civil disobedience. As Charles Ryrie, professor of Dallas Theological Seminary, wrote in 1970, "The didactic data of Scripture teaches complete civil obedience on the part of Christians and does not include any exceptions to this principle." The only exception he grants is "when the authority requires a believer to disobey the laws of God," such as in Peter's response to the Sanhedrin in Acts 4:19 and 5:29.

This exception illustrates, however, the uncertainty in applying the principle. There are a whole host of passages cited by advocates of civil disobedience who point out the counsel, "We ought to obey God rather than men" (Acts 5:29). The exceptions to the Romans 13 rule seem, in fact, rather widespread in Scripture. We hail Shadrach, Meshach, and Abed-nego who, when brought into conflict with Nebuchadnezzar's decree to worship the golden image, chose instead to disobey (Dan. 3:1-30). Daniel likewise disobeyed the laws of the Medes and the Persians (6:10). In Rabbinic scholar David Daube's volume, *Civil Disobedience in Antiquity,* he writes, "The oldest record in world literature of the spurning of a governmental decree occurs in the second book of Moses . . . this oldest instance of conscientious disobedience concerns a case of genocide." Daube refers to the story in Exodus 1:8—2:10 where the Hebrew midwives defied Pharaoh's order to kill all Hebrew males at birth and lied to Pharaoh to cover their tracks. The mothers "did not as the king of Egypt commanded them" (1:17).

There is also the story of Rahab, the harlot in Joshua 2, whose violations of the law are part of Israel's salvation story. The whole prophetic tradition seems to evidence no reluctance on the parts of the Jeremiahs, Ezekiels, and Elijahs to challenge civil authority. They not only call for faithfulness on the part of the king, but at times disobey kings or even participate in their overthrow.

The fundamental problem is not the principle, but the application. The principle seems clear enough: On those occasions when the government's command is clearly contrary to the Word of God, then it is the believer's duty to disobey the government. The problem is deciding what commands of government are contrary to the Word of God. Some extreme examples are clear, such as Nebuchadnezzar's command to bow down before idols or any command not to worship God.

But what about other government laws? Is the government requirement that one has to have a building permit for a church a law that warrants civil disobedience? What if those building permits are given rarely and prejudicially as, for example, in the Soviet Union? What about the government's requirement that private Christian schools use only teachers who graduated from state-accredited schools? What about a law using tax funds for abortion, or tax funds for the building of nuclear weapons, or a law permitting euthanasia?

In reality what one person perceives as a clear command of Scripture may be perceived by others as having nothing to do with religion at all. What one pastor views as a direct threat to the integrity of the church will be seen by another as a proper civil regulation. What one sees as a fundamental violation of biblical teaching will be seen by another as a proper political policy. The same uncertainties have invaded civil disobedience not simply out of a religious perspective, but out of a political one.

The issue of whether to participate in any civil disobedience is complex. Recent events indicate it is also urgent. While there is no debate about the legitimacy under certain circumstances of a refusal to obey the government, such acts must not be taken lightly. Not every governmental act which impedes Christian living or is inconvenient warrants such a response. Especially where such acts are designed to force government policy to change, the civil disobedience seems to need an even greater justification.

One writer suggests that "Christianity and the new state religion of America cannot peacefully coexist" and calls for Christian "rebels." Is this not more an advocacy of revolution than of mere obedience to conscience? Gary North suggests that, like the situation of Russian kulaks and German Jews, "There comes a time when continued patience is an inappropriate response ... the period of patience must be of a period of training." Are we not perilously close to turning the Christian community into a parapolitical organization which will vie for power, and use whatever context is necessary to establish its will?

In the weighing of factors, the following points must be carefully considered.

1. How directly and immediately does the opposed government action threaten an unequivocable biblical teaching? Is this an issue of an unequivocal threat to Christian faithfulness or is it rather a barrier which simply makes faithfulness to God more difficult?

2. What is the counsel of the Christian community in regard to the centrality of this issue and the appropriateness of this means?

3. To what extent have alternative remedies been exhausted within the democratic and political process?

4. What harms are likely to be brought about by engaging in civil disobedience and how do those balance out with the benefits to be gained? How likely is the act to create civil disruption and violence?

5. Can continuing respect for law and community be evident by the form that the civil disobedience will take?

6. To what extent will the "witness" of civil disobedience be properly understood by both the civil authorities and the public?

* * * * *

Check your interpretation of the preceding material with your answers to the following statements. Refusal to obey state laws is justified and appropriate in which of the following:

a. where state laws require immunization, but parents have a conscientious belief opposing such.

b. where state laws require parents to provide medical care for minors, but parents do not believe in using medical care because they trust God for their health.

c. where state law prohibits the importing without permission of religious materials, but a religious mission seeks to spread the Gospel by smuggling religious tracts.

d. when a sincere religious opponent of war wishes, contrary to the law, to selectively resist participation in war.

e. when a religiously and morally motivated protester refuses to pay taxes in opposition to government support of abortion.

f. when a church wishes to continue operation of a private school ordered closed by state courts for its refusal to use teachers with college degrees.

9

Parental
Rights

Would you side with the parent or against the parent in the following situations?

A parent wishes to gain legal custody of her 19-year-old daughter who has come under the influence of a religious cult group. She asks the court to permit her to remove her daughter against her will from the group.

* * * * *

The parents of a 3-year-old child decide, based on their religious beliefs, to refuse doctors permission to conduct an appendectomy. The parents say they trust in God's healing power. The doctor has appealed to the court for an order permitting the operation. (Would your opinion be different if the operation were to correct a cleft palate? Surgically improve hearing from 20 percent normal to 90 percent?)

* * * * *

Margie, a bright and seemingly well adjusted 17-year-old girl, seeks a court order granting her permission to attend a state university on a scholarship. Her parents have refused her permission. They do not believe girls ought to go to college, believe in any case she is too young, and further don't like the environment of the state college. Margie asks that she be legally emancipated from her parents' control.

* * * * *

Fran and Alex Honrashi are committed to strong discipline in the home. On four occasions this year, the parental punishment for their children's failure to eat their vegetables was confinement in their rooms without food for 24 hours. The children are also compelled to sit through all meals without speaking or be paddled. If the children receive any grades on papers or report cards below a B, they are confined to the house for one week. Teachers report the children seem highly withdrawn, anxious, and are achieving substantially below their apparent abilities. The Honrashis refuse to speak with school officials or other community authorities. The state seeks legal custody of the children, though leaving them in the home but under supervision with certain ground rules established by officials of the Department of Children and Family Services. The Honrashis cite their parental rights.

* * * * *

In 1979 Walter Polovchak made it clear he did not wish to return to the Soviet Union with his parents. Then 12 years old, Walter wanted to stay in the United States. Authorities refused to allow his parents to take him out of the country. Soviet officials and the parents complained about the violation of the rights of parents, and the American Civil Liberties Union filed suit in Chicago charging a violation of the parental rights of the Polovchaks.

Controversy raged in 1983 over whether the decision of parents to decline medical treatment for a newborn with a number of defects was a violation of the rights of the handicapped child. The "Baby Doe" case in Indiana raised a national controversy that led to the promulgation of a controversial federal rule requiring treatment of handicapped newborns and notices in hospitals inviting reports to authorities where there might be a failure to treat. A court struck down the rules.

In another case, a court ordered treatments for a child whose parents had chosen not to subject the child to the treatments which were of uncertain medical effect and had severe side effects.

Many Christian groups have expressed growing concern with government intervention into parental rights and the family arena.

Some are alarmists, viewing the government and courts as chief architects of a revolutionary overthrow of parental rights and family life.

In the early 1980s the National Christian Action Council summarized the feelings of many in a pamphlet:

Several years ago, the family was considered to be totally beyond the scope of government interference. The family was presumed to hold primary rights and responsibilities for rearing children, disciplining children, educating children, feeding children, clothing children, and housing children. . . . The child's spiritual welfare was a parental responsibility. The family passed along the cherished religious beliefs and values.

In days most of us still remember, to attack the family would be like attacking the flag. . . .

Times have changed.

Rather than a central moral and social unit, Oralee McGraw notes, "The family becomes instead a biological and sociological support mechanism that is only valuable to the extent the individual finds it so. If the family cannot provide self-fulfillment, the individual merely severs the family tie and moves on to the next 'passage' in the life cycle."

But it is by no means the government alone that is imposing the diminished significance of parenting and family life upon us. It may more centrally emerge from the whole nature of our focus on individualism, and the narcissism that naturally flows from it. The institutions of our society may be being undermined by our inordinate notions of freedom—conceived in purely individualistic terms.

We must also deal with the changes in family life resulting from our contemporary society. For good or ill, the emergence of industrialism, the movement of the population to the cities, the mobile society in which we live, and the separation of work from the home have created enormous social changes in family patterns—some positive, others negative. But the law and the courts are by no means the primary force shaping the nature of the family and the role of parents.

Fundamental Rights

At one level, family and parental rights are among the most highly regarded and cited liberties in the world. The Universal Declaration of Human Rights, Article 16, provides for the "right to marry and to found a family," and declares, "The family is the natural and fundamental group unit of society and entitled to protection by society and the state." Article 26 says, "Parents have a prior right to choose the kind of education that shall be given their children."

Similarly the International Covenant on Economic, Social, and Cultural Rights provides in Article 10 that "the widest possible protection and assistance should be accorded to the family." Article 17 of the International Covenant on Civil and Political Rights also declares, "No one shall be subjected to arbitrary and unlawful interference with his privacy, family, home, or correspondence" and requires "respect for the liberty of parents . . . to ensure the religious and moral education of their children in conformity with their own convictions."

Rights of families and parents are among society's most basic. These international commitments reflect an awareness that in the context of modern technology and ideology, the family may fall victim to social and political agendas.

The issues raised by the concerns about parental and family rights are sweeping, touching countless areas of controversy in public life today. Among the issues are such questions as:

- To what extent should the law affirmatively support family life and especially marriage?
- Do the tax laws penalize nuclear family units?
- Have no-fault divorce laws been an inevitable reflection of a changed society, or have they contributed to the ease and public acceptance of divorce, with disastrous consequences to our basic social institutions and to children?
- What rights should children have when their interests conflict with their parents'? Should parents have near unbridled authority regardless of the age of the child, until the child reaches 18?
- What rights should parents have regarding the activities of their children? For example, there has been controversy over the so-called "squeal rule" proposed by the Reagan administration

requiring any agency which receives federal funds to advise
parents of birth control prescriptions provided to minors.
• What is an appropriate response by government to the sweeping
tide of domestic violence in our society?

What about government efforts in these areas? Are they another expansion of dangerous government power? Are they motivated by values contrary to Christian thought? Or are they, however abusive at times, a necessary response to the tragic situations faced by our courts and agencies? These are complex areas, and far too broad for this brief chapter. But they are compelling issues which require attention from responsible leadership in our churches and communities.

Centrality of the Family and Parental Rights

The issue of the protection of parental rights and family autonomy is not a mere matter of individual liberty. More fundamentally, issues of parental rights and family rights raise essential issues about the character of society. Several arguments have been made for a vigorous protection of such liberties. Here are brief summaries of four arguments for protection of those rights:

1. Privacy. The family, especially in an increasingly technological and intrusive society, serves as a bastion of privacy against the claims of economic, social, and political institutions which constantly dehumanize and interfere with our identity and privacy. As such a refuge, the family serves a critical social and sociological role and is entitled to vigorous protection.

2. Nurture. There is increased evidence about the need for continuity of affectionate and stimulating relationships, and that such are essential for a child's normal development. This raises, as professor Bruce Hafen, writing in the *Michigan Law Review* notes, "serious doubts about the value of the dominant governmental service strategies of the past 20 years, whose planners have assumed that many family functions could be better performed by outside agencies." Hafen noted that recent data confirms how "vital the family is in the crucial arenas of individual motivation, personality structure, and creativeness." Hafen suggests these findings ought to give impetus to legal protection for formal families which can provide such stable environments. He concludes:

> Not all formal families are stable, nor do all necessarily provide wholesome continuity for their children. . . . But the commitments inherent in formal families do increase the likelihood of stability and continuity for children . . . [and] justify the denial of legal protection to unstable social patterns that threaten children's developmental environment.

Michael Novak has said that the family is the only "department of health, education, and welfare that works." Berger and Neuhaus put it this way: "Our preference for the parents over the experts is more than a matter of democratic conviction . . . virtually all parents love their children. Very few experts love, or can love, most of the children in their care. . . . In addition the parents, unlike the experts, have a long-term, open-ended commitment to the individual child."

3. Freedom. Because of the loneliness and alienation in our society, there is an increased need for what Edmund Burke cited as "the little platoon we belong to in society," a place which gives our lives meaning and identity. Without smaller associations, what some have called "mediating structures," there is an inevitable tendency for the state to assume the role of shaping and determining values and norms. In this sense there is a "political" role for the family in diminishing the tyranny of the state. Families assure pluralism. When the family ceases to function effectively, the state becomes all-powerful. Hafen suggests, "An essential element in maintaining a limited government is to deny state control over child-rearing."

Similarly with marriage David Lawrence observes, "The marriage bond . . . is the fundamental connecting link to Christian society. Break it and you will have to go back to the overwhelming dominance of the state."

4. Historical. Finally, it is significant that historically the family has been an essential sociological pattern. As Herbert Ratner, editor of *Child and Family Quarterly,* noted, "The traditional family, man and woman pairing in lifelong bond for the purpose of raising children to adulthood, is one of the most enduring and resilient realities of human history. Aberrations and deviations, innovations of one sort or another, come and go, but they never thrive or last. The traditional family has a habit of burying its undertakers."

Legal Concepts of Parental Rights

Historically the concept of parental rights over children was largely undebated. It wasn't that the law specifically provided for such rights; rather, they were assumed. Parents were the absolute masters, perhaps even owners, of children. The Roman legal principle *patria potestas* embodied the notion of children as the property of the father. Parental rights were really paternal rights with near absolute control. Child mortality was high, as much as 75 percent, and children were often perceived as replaceable.

Children had almost no legal or social status and child-rearing was often a task passed off to others. Children were abandoned, terrorized, often sexually abused (boy brothels existed in ancient Greece and Rome), and not infrequently killed. Children were thrown into rivers and left by roadsides. Though as early as A.D. 374 Rome had declared the killing of an infant murder, some reports indicate that as late as 1890, dead infants were a common sight in London.

The 16th century saw an emphasis on the need for the education of children and the strengthening of their character.

The special protection and status of children developed in the Western world in the 18th and 19th centuries, and the welfare of children became an increasing concern of society. The emphasis was not on children's *rights,* but on child *protection.* The 19th century saw numerous changes in both social and legal thought. Minimal duties were imposed on parents and sanctions for their violations. Several causes were at work including social concerns following industrialization. The two chief legal consequences were the child labor laws and the enactment of compulsory education statutes. These interferences with parental rights may seem both minor and reasonable today, but they were hotly contested then as improperly interfering with parents' rights. These 19th century developments did provide the basic concept that society has the right to limit parental rights.

American Law

American law has always given a strong theoretical protection of parental rights. Though such rights are not mentioned in the Constitution, courts recognized that inherent in the legal structure of our heritage and in the notion of a limited government was a protection of the family and parents.

Several cases have provided language strongly protective of parental rights and the centrality of the family.

In 1923, in striking down a Nebraska statute that barred the teaching of foreign languages in the public schools, the Supreme Court ruled that "the right of parents ... to instruct their children" is protected by the 14th Amendment. In 1925 the Supreme Court, in *Pierce vs. Society of Sisters,* struck down an Oregon law requiring parents to send their children to public schools and declared that the state could not seek to "standardize its children" and that "the child is not the mere creature of the state," but rather affirmed the rights of parents who "have the right, coupled with the high duty, to recognize and prepare him for additional obligations."

In 1934 in *Prince vs. Massachusetts* the Court wrote, "It is cardinal with us that the custody, care, and nurture of the child reside first in the parents, whose primary function and freedom include the preparation for obligations the state can neither supply nor hinder."

And in 1972 in *Yoder vs. Wisconsin* the Court, siding with Amish parents' objections to sending their children to high schools, stated, "The history and culture of Western civilization reflect a strong tradition of parental concern for the nurture and upbringing of children. The primary role of the parents in the upbringing of their children is now established beyond debate as an enduring American tradition."

Similar Supreme Court declarations have seen the family unit as central and protected. In 1965 in striking down the State of Connecticut's prohibition against the sale of birth control devices, Justice Goldberg declared,

> Certainly the safeguarding of the home does not follow merely from the sanctity of property rights. The home derives its preemi-

nence as the seat of family life. And the integrity of that life is somehow so fundamental that it has been found to draw to its protection the principles of more than one explicitly granted Constitutional right. . . . The entire fabric of the Constitution and the purposes that clearly underlie its specific guarantees demonstrate that the rights to marital privacy and to marry and raise a family are of a similar order and magnitude.

In striking down an ordinance in 1977 which in effect excluded grandparents from the definition of a family, the Court ruled, "The Constitution protects the sanctity of the family precisely because the institution of the family is deeply rooted in this nation's history and tradition. It is through the family that we inculcate and pass down many of our cherished values, moral and cultural."

The American Civil Liberties Union handbook on parental rights summarizes the significance of this commitment by noting, "The rights of parents and the rights of family integrity, in short, serve as a constitutional barrier to protect parents from unreasonable or unnecessary intrusion by the state into family life."

Not without Limits

This recognition of parental authority and privacy within the family is not unbridled. In a 1979 case, Chief Justice Warren Burger spoke of the law's reflection of "broad parental authority over minor children," but observed that "the state is not without constitutional control over parental discretion in dealing with children when their physical or mental health is jeopardized." But what justifies an intrusion or interference?

Whenever there is a fundamental right in issue (such as freedom of speech, religion, or family privacy), the state may interfere only by showing a "compelling interest" and the courts will review such claims with "strict scrutiny." But what constitutes such a "compelling interest"? What interests of the government are legitimate? Who decides?

In certain cases the results are not surprising. For example, the courts have traditionally found a compelling state interest when a child's life is threatened, for example, by parental refusal to permit lifesaving medical treatment such as a transfusion. When a child's physical safety is imminently threatened, the "compelling interest" seems clear. But what about such principles as "mental health"? That's more slippery.

Children's Rights Movement—The Kiddie-Libbers

While the 19th century focused on certain necessary limits of parental rights for the protection of children, the mid- and late-20th century has seen the emergence of the concept of children's *rights*. Those with more radical notions have often been labeled "kiddie-libbers."

In 1959 the United Nations adopted a declaration that "mankind owes the child the best it has to give." The UN Declaration listed a number of things "mankind owes to the child," among them the right to affection, right to adequate nutrition, right to a name and nationality, right to special care if handicapped, right to be among the first to receive relief in times of disaster, right to learn to be a useful member of society and to develop individual abilities. It didn't seem a radical or bizarre list.

But it was Richard Farson's *Birthrights* (Penguin Books) which went much further, speaking of the right to self-determination, sexual freedom, economic power, and alternative home environments. For Farson and others who have followed this lead, such as Holt's *Escape from Childhood,* the emphasis is not on the duties of parents and society to *nurture* children. Rather, the shift is from nurturance to "self-determination"—giving children the right to determine what's good for themselves. As Farson himself declared, "The issue of self-determination is at the heart of children's liberation."

It wasn't hard to see how such a notion could easily include an assault on traditional family structures and parental authority. Parental values which "inhibit" freedom would, for such persons, be anathema. Parents are perceived as getting in the way of their children's moral and religious emancipation. When lower courts have sustained denial of notice to parents by arguing that to bring the parents in might interfere with freedom of choice, one does indeed have cause for concern.

The reaction to children's rights advocacy has been less than enthusiastic from many religious communities. When the UN declared 1979 the Year of the Child, many religious groups warned of its intent. Some were vehement. The *Gospel Truth* periodical called it "Satan's Attack on the Family," and Senator Orrin Hatch feared it would become an "all-out assault on our traditional family structure."

From a legal perspective, however, the development of children's rights has been slow. While children's rights of privacy in the areas of abortion and contraception have been protected, and the rights of juveniles to due process of law in both civil and criminal cases has been clearly set forth, the courts have not gone off wholesale in discovering or manufacturing children's rights. The problems of state intervention in families emerge in much more complex contexts than the abstract advocacy of children's rights which produces much rhetoric but little guidance.

What disturbs many conservatives about the trends today? Why are many commentators nervous? Two elements of the contemporary scene seem to raise these apprehensions: first, the courts; and second, state intrusion into family affairs.

The Courts. Despite the affirmation of parental rights in many court cases, the concern with judicial holdings is growing. The concern is partly with certain specific decisions which seem to evidence a narrowing of parental rights. For example, in a series of decisions the courts have severely restricted the rights of parents in areas related to abortion and sexuality. In *Danforth vs. Planned Parenthood* the Supreme Court struck down the veto power of parents over a minor's abortion decision, holding that the privacy rights of the minor were more important. It justified the infringement on parental rights by declaring that in such a setting the "very existence of the pregnancy already has fractured the family structure." In *Belotti vs. Baird (II)* the minor is permitted to go to court without consultation or notice to parents. Lower courts have struck down almost every attempt by legislatures to provide any parental notice in such circumstances.

More than the specific decisions, however, is concern over the court's tendency to view the granting of parental rights as a delegation of power from the state rather than as being inherent. That is, the court increasingly sees an expanding arena as legitimate for government review, and merely chooses not to exercise power rather than being devoid of the power in the first instance. The concept of parental rights is thus more and more open to review in each case. One is less and less sure that the court will not find a "compelling state interest."

State intrusion into family affairs. The courts, however, are really not the chief concern. They tend to act only when some clash occurs between claimed parental rights and some government agency. More disturbing to many is the increasing degree to which other branches of government become involved in matters of high concern to family integrity and privacy—and often do so with little recognition of our concern for the interests of the parents.

The growing involvement of schools in such areas as sex education, life education, and values teaching tends to inevitably move schools into the roles of parent substitutes. Radical commentators even openly indicate that one of the educational tasks they see upon us is reshaping the way children think—away from the teachings of their parents.

Every bureaucracy seeks to expand its influence and be somewhat messianic in its claims. We see that not only in education, but in other state agencies as well. As critical a function as such programs play in our society, they dare not be permitted to shift the centrality of the family unit. And as a society becomes more pluralistic, they dare not be permitted to take their own notions of parenting, psychological well-being, and nurture and turn them into norms and standards for every family or family ministry. The danger is that as a secular philosophy becomes increasingly perceived as "right" and normative, it becomes the standard, and then soon becomes one of those "compelling state interests" which courts will find more important than parental rights.

A Secularist Perspective

Of course, behind the courts' decisions and the legislative programs is a point of view—a philosophy. The difficult task is to carefully sort out those aspects of government policy and public viewpoint which express deep and legitimate concerns (even if some might disagree with the specific means of implementing them) from those approaches which run fundamentally counter to Christian perspectives. In this connection there are two quite different legitimate concerns. The first is with the substance or content of government policy. One may, for example, be quite concerned about the values taught in a sex education curriculum which reflect Planned Parenthood's philosophy of sexuality, or about a policy barring state licensed agencies from any corporal punishment of children. The second concern, however, is not so much with the *content* as with the *authority*. The problem here is not with what decisions or policies are adopted, but the danger of a society relinquishing to government the *power* to increasingly invade the turf. The questions here are about jurisdiction. As already noted, there is a danger well noted in history of totalitarian government. The most dangerous totalitarian is the one who insists he is going to "do good," is going to "help" or "save" you. He may honestly believe that, but it makes it all the more a threat to liberty.

Many critics of state agencies have vastly overstated the dangers in these agencies' involvements, and they have used the most extreme instances of abuse of power to color the entire agency. But even a much more balanced appraisal must acknowledge the inherent risks in state intrusion into family life through increased public control of education, expansion of government day care programs, adoption of philosophic viewpoints in educational curriculum dealing with moral and values issues, child abuse hot lines, etc.

Areas of Controversy
Two major areas which have resulted in substantial controversy illustrate the tensions over parental rights versus state rights: educational issues and domestic violence, especially child abuse.

Educational issues. Education has produced parental rights disputes in the context of both public and private education. Parents have raised issues of parental rights in seeking exemption for their children from participation in various components of public education which they feel interfere with their parental prerogatives. Most commonly this occurs in such areas as values clarification and sex education. When the content of such courses is contrary to the parents' values and morals, what rights do they have to bar the programs, or at least obtain exemptions from participation? While many state statutes or school board policies do provide for exemption from such programs on religious grounds, courts have seldom found an absolute parental or religious right to such exemption. Instead, they apply the "compelling state interest" test and a few courts have declined to hold that parental or free exercise of religious rights prevail over state required courses.

In the private school arena, parental rights have become hotly debated in the growing movement toward home education— teaching your children at home rather than sending them to either public or private schools. Recent books, such as Raymond and Dorothy Moore's *Home-Spun Schools* (Word Books), have advocated that parents assume the responsibility for teaching their own children, especially in the early school years. Such attempts may, however, run afoul of state laws. Thus, challenges are set up between the state's conception of what fulfills the compulsory education requirement and the parents' rights to educate their children.

Court battles have raged in many states with the final legal issues unresolved. While some courts have found fundamental parental and/or religious rights to teach one's children at home provided one can demonstrate a bona fide and effective educational program, other courts have been more restrictive, requiring strict compliance with state statutes which may or may not provide directly or indirectly for such home schools. Several legal groups, including the Christian Legal Society, have published material for parents on the legal aspects of this element of parental and religious liberty.

Domestic violence. In November 1983, *Newsweek* featured the "unspeakable crimes" that are "being yanked out of the shadows." The article noted the growing awareness of the enormity of private domestic violence, including child abuse and battered wives. The statistics are shocking. One-fifth of all murders are committed by loved ones. The statistics are felt, however, to reveal only the tip of the iceberg since much domestic violence by its nature goes unreported. Experts are unsure themselves of whether the number of women beaten by their husbands is 2 million or closer to 6 million. But whatever the exact figures, private violence is coming into the open. Over 2,000 women are beaten to death annually. As many as 6 millon women may be physically abused by their spouses annually. Battery is the single major cause of injury to women. The problem is exacerbated by the reluctance of the victims to report the crimes, pursue charges if they have been reported, or take immediate steps to extract themselves from the dangerous conditions. As Jane Tolliver, with the Atlanta YMCA battered women's program noted, women are frequently told that they can, if they stick it out, change the men who beat them. Twenty-five percent of women's suicide attempts are preceded by a prior history of wife beating.

Child abuse reports are growing. Reports between 1976 and 1981 by the American Humane Society increased from 413,000 to 851,000 and climbed another 12 percent in 1982. As *Newsweek* observed, "The wall of silence is breaking down." Neighbors and relatives are more willing to report child abuse to local authorities. Public awareness has grown. Polls show a dramatic increase from 10 percent to 90 percent in the sense of the public that child abuse is a serious national problem.

Sexual abuse of children is far more common than most people realize. Some victims have begun to tell their stories, such as Linda Holliday in her autobiography, *Silent Scream*. Dr. Annette Ficker, a pediatrician at Children's Hospital National Medical Center in Washington, D.C. noted that half of the 600 child abuse cases handled there each year are of sexual abuse often involving children 2 years of age and younger.

In response to the growing awareness, community organizations and state officials have developed a variety of services including hot lines for parents who are losing control. Mandatory reporting laws have been adopted in several states which require various professionals such as doctors and teachers to report suspected cases of child abuse. Names reported are then placed in a national confidential register—a computer bank to allow law enforcement officials to check patterns of complaints. The hot lines are anonymous and result in immediate investigations by state officials into allegations. Parents Anonymous, patterned after Alcoholics Anonymous, has been developed for chronic offenders.

But, as urgently needed as some of these responses may have been, they have created a storm of controversy. Civil rights groups have complained about the concept of anonymous tipsters alleging child abuse with resulting investigations by state officials. The parents accused have no right to know who has alleged the abuse. They do not have the right to confront the witnesses. Some statistics seem to show that a substantial portion of such hot line tips are calls from angry neighbors or jealous suitors who use the device to create further anguish. When such tips combine with officious state agencies, the potentials for abuse are substantial. Numerous outrageous stories of state interference, arrests, and long-term investigations have been recounted where there was no substance at all.

The child abuse arena has been further muddied by definitional problems. When one focuses not only on physical abuse but emotional abuse, the issues become fuzzy. Many public officials view any corporal punishment as inhumane and borderline child abuse. Private religiously motivated child care institutions have been threatened with loss of state licenses for applying corporal punishment, even without any claim that it is excessive. But who decides those questions? In 1979 Sweden made it a crime to strike a child or to treat a child in an inhumane way.

These issues of parental rights illustrate the difficult and sensitive interplay of values, legal rights, social concepts, and institutional structures in modern society.

10

How to
Find a Lawyer

For many people, obtaining legal counsel and relying on that counsel is a frustrating and fearsome experience. Even calling a lawyer produces great anxiety. *What is it going to cost? What am I getting myself into? How do I know if the lawyer is any good?* All these questions, compounded with the mystique about lawyers, legal language, and legal institutions, have created great reluctance and fear about approaching lawyers.

A woman complained bitterly that after meeting with a lawyer to discuss the possibility of a legal claim regarding an injury, and then making a subsequent phone call to discuss it further, the attorney had forwarded a bill for the time spent in both the meeting and the phone call. The lady was outraged that there would be a charge for such a preliminary discussion, doubly outraged that a phone call would result in a charge, and concluded, "And I thought he was a Christian."

The matters of finding legal help, developing an appropriate relationship with that legal counsel, being satisfied with the lawyer's work and fees are frequent problems. Perhaps a few suggestions will help in these areas.

Do You Really Need Legal Help?

There is a legal maxim, "For every wrong there is a remedy." Don't believe it. Despite the increasing number of laws that touch every area of our lives and the vast expansion of civil lawsuits to gain redress for wrongs, many situations have no legal remedy. Indeed, many people seem to have experienced great injustices. Systems and structures of society seem to have almost conspired against them and they find themselves without work, with disrupted families, with legal liabilities. These people wonder if the American legal system, with its commitments to equal protection, due process, and civil rights, can't help them. Often the answer is no. The law is often helpless to heal the most critical pains. The wrongs that many people have experienced may have little or nothing to do with the law. In some situations there is perhaps a legal remedy, but it is not a satisfying solution. The complexity and cost of our legal system creates barriers to many people's attempts to use the law. In California, for example, the suggestion is that if the financial elements of a claim are not at least $5,000 it is not "worth it," at least in economic terms, to pursue legal remedies. At the purely economic level, in many cases the formal remedy is not a practical one. You might have a case; you may even win. But you may not come out ahead financially.

For a Christian, it's also important to weigh other costs—use of time, consumption of energies, diversion from other priorities, basic attitudes. Check yourself with these questions:

- If I had three years to live, how much of that time would I spend on a lawsuit on this matter?
- How will pursuing this claim affect my spiritual life?
- Am I really pursuing justice and seeking a proper resolution of a dispute, or am I motivated by resentment and revenge?

Surely, however, there are times when people *do* need legal counsel. One such situation is obvious: litigation such as when a person is brought into court by another party either through a criminal or a civil procedure, or other contexts where the legal dimensions of a problem require special professional help. In such situations almost everyone recognizes the need for legal counsel. While the legal system provides that persons may represent themselves, it is usually not advisable. Even if a person were familiar with the legal process, the use of legal counsel adds an element of objectivity and analysis that is often lost when a person represents himself.

People also need legal counsel to help them manage their financial affairs. Lawyers are not mere adversaries, but counselors. In our society, a lawyer's function is to help people avoid legal problems rather than to control those problems once they emerge. Lawyers are equipped to give special counsel in organizing one's financial affairs, managing an estate so as to minimize tax liabilities, looking at alternative forms of business organizations, reviewing the character of one's assets for tax minimization purposes, etc. Even novice law students realize that careful legal planning can substantially improve a person's business or financial effectiveness and that the attorney's fee may be saved many times over. Careful legal planning can avoid surprises and even disasters.

In earlier generations, many persons went through life without ever consulting a lawyer. But with the problems we face today with buying and selling property, writing wills, and completing tax forms, it is much riskier to avoid legal advice.

Save a Buck: "Do-It-Yourself" Law
There is a trend in our society for persons to handle their own legal problems. Norman Dacey's *How to Avoid Probate* (Crown Books) was the first in a string of books which purports to provide all the guidance you need to form your own corporations, file divorce actions, and otherwise save enormous legal fees.

Many general books give an overview of the law. These are in fact quite helpful. The Reader's Digest publication *You and the Law* gives a general framework of the law in such areas as personal rights, property rights, negligence suits, going to court, automobile accidents, contracts, family law, employee rights, social security, wills and estates, etc. Specialized books on specific areas of law are helpful too. *The Battle for Religious Liberty* (David C. Cook Publishing Co.) provides an overview of the complex area of religious liberty, including the rights of Christian teachers in public schools, the rights of students, legal issues related to private schools, rights to engage in public evangelism, etc. Richard Hammar's *Pastor, Church and Law* is a similar summary of church law. The Christian Legal Society's *Public School Policy Manual* provides an important resource for school principals, attorneys, and parents on issues related to public school policies that affect religion and values.

However, these general summaries and the specific "do-it-yourself" guides must be used with caution. Not only does the law frequently change either by judicial decisions or by acts of the legislature, but the law is indeed as complex as people accuse it of being. A lawyer must not only know the legal rules and principles, but he must know how to apply them with precision to specific cases. Often what appears to be a relatively minor fact will substantially change the applicable law. What may appear as a "simple" matter in a legal book or in a do-it-yourself manual, will, upon greater examination, not be simple at all. It is with considerable risk that persons rely on general advice and fail to examine the applicable state and local laws or use those laws to their benefit. This is precisely the task of the lawyer.

Finding an Honest Lawyer
A lawyer-client relationship is essentially built upon trust. It is critical that the client have confidence in the lawyer's ability and integrity. It is not surprising, therefore, that persons often find it difficult to choose a lawyer. Scanning the *Yellow Pages* or calling the number flashing on the television screen hardly seems an adequate way to pick someone who must become a trusted colleague, a possessor of secrets, a trustee of our assets, and perhaps a defender of our liberty.

People should not agree to be represented or to retain any counsel unless they are satisfied that a trust relationship exists. For this reason, the best way to identify legal counsel is really by word-of-mouth referrals.

Other sources of referrals are large associations that people may belong to, such as churches. Hardly any large church is without some lawyers in its membership, and certainly local pastors would be familiar with the lawyers in a community and their reputations. Other community religious, business, or professional associations may also offer referrals. Another source of help is the local County Bar Association, which usually has a formal or informal lawyer referral service. For persons with severely limited incomes, such Bar Associations may have referral systems for indigent clients.

Where there is an urgent need for legal assistance and a person is truly unable to pay the usual legal fees, many lawyers will waive or subtantially reduce their fees. Too often, however, people for whom the fees are simply inconvenient or difficult expect free counsel.

Legal aid clinics are often available for providing legal assistance for persons who fall below a certain minimum income. These clinics are usually, however, limited to handling civil cases. They are often helpful in dealing with such matters as social security claims, unemployment compensation, landlord-tenant disputes, and consumer credit. Criminal defense for indigent clients may be handled by either full-time "public defenders" or by court-appointed counsel. Every person criminally charged with a serious offense is entitled to legal representation, and if they cannot afford it, it will be provided for them by the state.

In the case of small civil claims (often under $500, or in some jurisdictions, up to $1,000 or $2,000), one may bring a civil claim in small claims courts. These informal courts provide an opportunity for a person to bring a claim against another individual or corporation. The process is made simple enough that one does not need legal counsel. (Though if the corporation is the defendant, it may be represented by an attorney. A private party usually must represent himself.) No special legal knowledge is needed. Assistance is provided in filling in the basic forms required.

Do You Need a Christian Lawyer?

One frequent request people make is for a Christian lawyer. We often wonder what they mean by such a request. Do they feel that the legal issues are of such a nature that they require a person who is aware of the Christian community, its structures, traditions, and theology? Or do they want to be assured that the attorney is a person of integrity and honesty, who perhaps also shares their particular values and therefore might proceed in the case in a manner consistent with Christian commitment? These might be quite valid interests in choosing an appropriate attorney. Sometimes, however, I believe that people who ask for a Christian lawyer really want a cheap, if not *free,* attorney.

For anyone seeking legal help, the first concern really ought to be with the lawyer's competence and trustworthiness. These are by no means the exclusive province of Christians. I'd rather have a competent secularist lawyer than an incompetent Christian one. Not all Christian lawyers are necessarily the best legal counselors on a specific matter.

Lawyers, perhaps, are delighted to revel in the myth that the mere fact of being a lawyer makes one an expert in every area of law. Many people seem to assume that the possession of a law degree indicates not only general competence, but competence in virtually every area. But in fact, the practice of law has become increasingly specialized. While historically formal specializations in law were limited to such areas as patent law and admiralty, many states are recognizing other specialities as well, such as family law and tax law. Even where states do not formally certify specialists, it is quite common, particularly in metropolitan areas, for lawyers to limit their practices to certain specific topics. The general practitioner certainly still exists, but even this lawyer is likely to refer specialized and complex cases to attorneys who deal specifically with those areas of the law. This increased specialization ought to make potential clients careful that their lawyers are competent in the particular areas where they need legal help. The friendly family attorney who wrote your mother's will may not be the best lawyer for the church's battle with the Internal Revenue Service, or for your corporation's consideration of the sale of securities. When you speak with an attorney about possible representation, ask him about his experience in the specific areas at issue. Do not hesitate to get alternative opinions. It's *your* case and *your* money.

Lawyer Fees

Few subjects are as sensitive as the matter of lawyers' fees. A bill of several hundred dollars for a few sheets of paper seems outrageous. When we read of an enormous judgment in a medical malpractice case with a paraplegic defendant and note that the attorneys received perhaps 40 or even 50 percent of all the funds the jury awarded for the care of the victim, we wonder about the justice of it.

We must understand several important points about lawyers' fees. First, most lawyer-fee problems with clients emerge from a failure of the lawyer and the client to each take responsibility at the first meeting for thorough and open discussion of the financial arrangements. Too often it appears that both sides are afraid to raise financial questions. Thus, it is easy for misunderstandings to exist about what kinds of actions entail a fee, whether there are fees for preliminary consultations, how the fees are calculated, and when the fees are payable. One benefit about the increasing openness in lawyer advertising rules is to perhaps encourage more candid discussion of costs. When consulting an attorney, it is appropriate to inquire in an initial conversation on the phone as well as in any office consultation, the nature and scope of the legal fees.

Second, except in the most routine matters (remember that what *appears* routine may not be) it is often difficult for lawyers to be absolutely firm about the cost of legal representation. While the client may chiefly think in terms of a "task," such as the preparation of a will, incorporation of an organization, sale of a piece of property, or obtaining a federal tax exemption, the attorney usually thinks more in terms of time. What the lawyer esentially has to "sell" is time. The time that a given legal matter takes is often uncertain at the beginning. It is unclear because of the uncertain nature of the task, and because, particularly in the case of litigation, the time required may be determined by other parties. Until an attorney has begun to investigate both the facts and the law, the total amount of time that may be required will only be a rough estimate.

In an adversary relationship, opposing parties may engage in extensive discovery which involves taking depositions and answering interrogatories. There may be numerous preliminary hearings. All of this combines to create considerable uncertainty regarding what legal representation may cost. That is very frustrating to the client who would like to know at least what the range is. While an attorney may be able to indicate that a given matter might run approximately $350, except in a most routine matter, he will usually caution that his estimate assumes there will be no complications in the case or in the response of other parties.

Third, it is important to recognize how a lawyer's time is spent. The legal fees are usually based on the number of hours spent on tasks relating to the client's case. This time involves *meeting* with the client, *researching* applicable laws, *thinking* of and *planning* the best way to respond to a legal problem, *drafting* documents, *consulting* with other persons (such as experts in a field, court officials, government agencies, or the opposing counsel), *conferring* with parties or opponents, *conversing* by phone, and sometimes *appearing* in court. Phone conversations occasionally produce significant misunderstanding. The client is often surprised that there is a bill for a 10-minute phone call. But since the lawyer functions primarily in terms of time, whether that conversation with a client occurs in an office or on the phone is really not significant. A good bit of the consultation which a lawyer will do will involve phone conversations. It's far more efficient and usually takes less time than if the consultation were to occur in the office.

Fourth, while most of the work will be done on an hourly basis, there are two other financial arrangements which may be appropriate. In some situations, where the matter is routine, there may be a flat rate. This is most common in uncontested divorces, simple wills, or cases involving traffic violations. The more common exceptional arrangement is the contingent fee. Contingent fee cases are those in which the attorney's fees (not including out-of-pocket costs) will be paid only if the lawsuit is successful. Such fees are not usually applicable in general consultation, such as business planning. Contingent fees are also improper in any criminal case; a lawyer may not ethically enter into a relationship where he is paid only if the verdict is not guilty. In civil cases, contingent fees are quite common. Notable common examples are civil suits for negligent injury.

One purpose for allowing such fees is to enable the client, who could not afford the extensive costs involved in civil litigation, to obtain legal representation from an attorney; the attorney's compensation being dependent on successful litigation. Often, but not always, compensation where the suit is successful will exceed the fees that would have been generated by an hourly rate. But in those cases where the suit is unsuccessful or the judgment awarded is quite low, the attorney may be virtually uncompensated for substantial work. Thus the apparently high contingent fees (frequently one-third if the matter is solved without going to trial and 40 percent or even higher if it does go to trial) are intended to represent some balance. Some states have put caps on the scope of legal fees in such cases and are subject to state Bar Association rules regarding fair and reasonable fees. (Ethical rules make it clear that the contingency fee arrangement is not intended to be the norm, and in any event, lawyers are to advise clients regarding the financial options which exist.)

Fifth, while the concern about exorbitant legal fees is often legitimate, many Christians wrongly assume that Christian lawyers ought to charge other Christians substantially less or provide free service. Christian lawyers are not, despite the apparent belief, fed by ravens who appear in the evening. Christian attorneys, as much as Christian plumbers, Christian printers, Christian factory workers, and Christian teachers are entitled to a fair and reasonable compensation for their work.

Finally, problems occasionally arise because lawyers do not make clear to their clients the difference between legal fees and out-of-pocket costs, which lawyers may advance but which are ultimately the client's responsibility. Frequently in the course of legal representation, the attorney will pay recording fees, filing fees, court costs, or state fees associated with such matters as incorporation. These out-of-pocket costs are not included in the legal fees. They are, however, billed to the client. Again, open discussion of the scope of these fees at the outset of legal representation may avoid confusion.

If You're Unhappy with Your Attorney

Many people may not realize it, but the attorney/client relationship may be terminated by the client at any point. While the client will remain liable for the services already rendered, the mere fact that one has entered into an agreement to retain an attorney does not require the person to continue in that relationship.

Of course, many times people become unhappy with lawyers for the wrong reasons. The interminable delays that are so much a part of the legal process may not be the lawyer's fault. Frequently clients blame their attorneys for inattention to their cases, or even deliberate delays to enhance the legal fees.

At times, clients blame attorneys for the result. Recently, while riding a bus from the circuit court house in Chicago back to my office, I overheard a conversation between a woman and a bus driver. The woman indicated that she had called a couple of attorneys in order to hire a lawyer for her son who'd been charged with several serious felonies. The woman indicated that one attorney wanted $5,000 and said he felt the defendant could get off with serving no more than a year in jail. The second attorney, however, wanted $10,000, but guaranteed that the woman's son would serve no jail time. "He promised," she told the driver. She naturally chose the man who could guarantee the most. But, of course, no lawyer can guarantee the results of litigation.

There are appropriate reasons for clients to be concerned about the adequacy of their legal counsel. Some lawyers are notorious for their failure to be responsive to client inquiry, to advise clients on the progress of the matter being handled, to return phone calls, and to neglect similar aspects of the relationship that evidence the trust placed in them. A client has every right to expect that a lawyer will be diligent in his work and will regularly advise him of the case's progress. Persistent patterns of failure to do so may well justify the client's desire for a new lawyer.

Many of these problems can be avoided if the client and lawyer both recognize the importance of clear communication and mutual understanding. Then the client is able to make informed decisions. And remember, the client is the one with the claim or the potential liability—not the attorney. The lawyer offers counsel, suggests options, and may determine trial strategies. But decisions about whether to sue, whether to settle, whether to "cop a plea," or whether to proceed with a claim are the *client's* choices. The client has the responsibility to make clear to his attorney what he wants.

11

How Dare
You Sue!

It was with some consternation that the early Tuesday morning Bible study group of lawyers suddenly encountered 1 Corinthians 6:1: "Does any one of you, when he has a case against his neighbor, dare to go to law before the unrighteous, and not before the saints?" (NASB) There it was—bold, clear, decisive: "How dare you sue one another." No beating around the bush.

As the lawyers discussed the verse, they noted, of course, that the implications were not easily avoided. That is, not easily avoided in *theory.* In *practice,* of course, people were avoiding them daily. The attorneys represented many Christian clients: landlords, tenants, entrepreneurs, contractors, builders, doctors, architects, even Christian organizations. Many of their clients seemed motivated by biblical authority. But none seemed to pay much attention to Paul's question in 1 Corinthians 6:1.

Paul suggests in the passage that it brings discredit on the Christian community when a believer takes another believer to court. Paul demands that instead of going to pagan Roman courts, the Christian community should use the resources of the church. "Is there not even one among you wise enough to resolve the dispute?" (See v. 5.) Paul anticipates the answer of some frustrated disputant and suggests if it comes to that, it is better to be defrauded (v. 7). Better to be ripped off, cheated, or abused, than to take a Christian brother to court.

Biblical Avoidance, 101

If anything is clear in Christian history, it is that we have learned ways to avoid clear Bible teaching. It has become quite a skill—not a skill taught in formal training; you can't take "Avoidance, 101." It is taught much more persuasively by observing Christian conduct. Countless people have developed this skill to such a degree that they can take straightforward words like, "How dare you sue one another," and turn them into mere suggestions, or make them so cluttered with exceptions and caveats as to swallow up the rule in the exception.

One common avoidance technique is to insist that the other party is not a believer, therefore the passage does not apply. The beauty of this technique is you can continue to insist on the authority of Scripture and the duty to be obedient to it, but merely point out that it doesn't apply in *your* particular case. When asked for the evidence that the other party is not a believer, you answer, "No one who does anything such as they did to me could be a Christian." It's a self-defining exception.

Another attempt to avoid the clear teaching of the passage is to use some ruse that seeks a "deeper meaning." The technique goes something like this. You approach your local pastor or seminary professor and suggest that while the text you have is quite clear ("how dare you sue one another"), you are seeking the truth from the original Greek. What is the *real* meaning of this text? What did Paul *really* want to say?

Sadly, such techniques totally fail us with 1 Corinthians 6. In the Greek this text really means, "How dare you sue one another."

Un-American Activities

Whatever the biblical teachings, they have had little impact on American society or the church. We are inundated by "lexophobia," the lawsuit disease. Jerold Auerbach suggested, "At the first sign of trouble, an American reaches for his hired gun and files a lawsuit." Despite all the pleas for alternatives, Auerbach sees little change. He says the propensity to the lawsuit is "unlikely to recede unless Americans decide to become un-American."

In fact, lexophobia seems to be a rampaging virus. In fact, from 1940 to 1982, federal civil court cases grew from 35,000 to 238,875 a year. The federal courts of appeal increased from 2,800 cases to 26,000 cases in approximately the last 30 years. Each year 7.2 million civil and criminal suits are filed.

Very few of the lawsuits make the news. Some that do seem quite humorous, perhaps even frivolous. When Wendy Potasnik, a 9-year-old girl from Carmel, Indiana, sued Cracker Jack, she made the national network news. Wendy's complaint was that as she desperately looked among the caramel corn, alas, she had been ripped off—abused by corporate negligence, another victim of big business—for there was no prize. As Wendy said, "Since I bought their product because of their claim, they broke a contract with me."

Other lawsuits are less funny. Something seems amiss when a jury awards a former Illinois Supreme Court Justice, Thomas Klucynski, and his wife, $208,000 for being "bumped" from an air flight. Or what of the 10-year-old boy who successfully sued his school for not preventing him from playing hooky. While skipping school, the young boy was injured by a motorcycle and successfully held the school liable for his injuries. They should have kept a tighter leash on him. It reminds me of the classic story of the child who murdered his parents and pled in court for mercy because he was an orphan.

Few complaints can compete with one filed by a New York attorney against General Motors. The class action suit was filed on behalf of "all persons everywhere now alive and all future unborn generations." It's not surprising he asked $6 trillion in damages. For audacity, one might note the divorce action recently reported by Johnny Carson's wife who sued for support. She modestly asked for $220,000 a month. But so as not to be thought greedy, she filed a family budget. The budget included:

- $37,065 a month to buy jewelry and furs
- $21,625 a month to run her Bel-Air mansion
- $4,930 a month for contributions to charities
- $155 a month to send flowers to people
- $1,200 a month to pay club membership dues

- $1,110 a month for payments to American Express
- $2,695 monthly for travel and lodging
- over $12,000 a month to buy gifts for friends and relatives

But lawsuits are essentially not funny at all. Behind them rest anger, bitterness, unforgiveness, and resentment. And the judicial process, intended to provide justice, often exacerbates ill will, drives parties further apart, wastes resources, and consumes enormous spiritual and psychological energies.

One need only look at an area like family law to recognize how tragically helpless the courts are. The depth of frustration was tragically illustrated in 1983 in the domestic courts of Chicago. In a domestic relations case, a frustrated petitioner in a wheelchair, upon having a motion denied for the appointment of new counsel, removed a revolver from under a blanket covering his legs, shot and killed Judge Henry Gentile, and then shot and killed his estranged wife's attorney.

Why Lexophobia?

Why such a flood of litigation? Behind the explosion of litigation is a great sense of the loss of community, an inordinate focus on rights without a correlative sense of duties, a tendency to try to put financial value on every harm and wrong, the failure of our social institutions to provide support for people who hurt and suffer, and our lack of capacity to observe even minor wrong.

Certain aspects of the expanding number of lawsuits reflect legitimate concerns for justice. New areas of the law have expanded, contributing to explosions of litigation. At times such litigation has been essential to secure human rights, to hold manufacturers liable for their clear negligence, to protect the environment, and to call people to account for repeated gross violations of law and social duties. But the litigious spirit of American life extends far beyond these legitimate concerns for justice.

Isn't There a Better Way?

So sweeping is the flood of litigation and the types of cases now brought before the courts, that legal professionals are pleading for alternatives. Chief Justice Warren Burger in an address at the

American Bar Association Convention in 1982 queried, "Isn't there a better way?" Burger noted the failure of litigation to truly resolve human conflict. He insisted the "result is often drained of much of its value because of the time lapse, the expense, and the emotional stress." He cited Judge Learned Hand's comment: "I should dread a lawsuit beyond almost anything else short of sickness and death." Doctors have even been known to speak of "litigation neuroses" as they observe patients whose very health is threatened by the litigious spirit.

But litigants aren't the only victims. In a fascinating article by Wayne Brazil, the law professor notes the "infectiousness" of the viruses of litigation practice. Deploring the pressures that have existed in his law practice from his "role as a combatant," he decries the manipulation, intimidation, and exploitation that have occurred. He found himself exploiting the vulnerability and the weaknesses of others as a "full-time professional combatant." He felt "lessened, cheapened, degraded." When he wanted to be "open, candid, cooperative," he was "closed, self-conscious, contrived." He insisted, "Competitive and adversarial pressures that prompt such practices are so inherent in our system of dispute resolution that some forms of predatory, deceitful, and manipulative behavior seem inevitable." He concluded, "Woe to the peaceful. Woe to those to whom constant competition is not comfortable and to whom victory is less important than justice."

Settle It in the Church

Matthew 18 suggests that the church is responsible to settle legal disputes.

> If your brother sins against you, go and tell him his fault, between you and him alone. If he listens to you, you have gained your brother. But if he does not listen, take one or two others along with you, that every word may be confirmed by the evidence of two or three witnesses. If he refuses to listen to them, tell it to the church; and if he refuses to listen to even the church, let him be to you as a Gentile and a tax collector (Matt. 18:15-17, RSV).

The church is the place for legal peacemaking, not simply because these verses require it, but because the church is sensitive to larger issues in a person's life. The church is sensitive to human personality, to feelings of hurt, resentment, anger, and bitterness. The church can touch not only the legal issues, but the spiritual dimensions as well. The church can move not merely to adjudication, but to reconciliation. The church invites not simply restitution, but restoration. In its declarations of forgiveness, the church provides confession, renewal, and the capacity to set aside, to release, and to be made whole. The church has the resources of the Christian community which can gather around, exercising not only gifts of judgment, but gifts of peacemaking, caring, restoring, and comforting.

Strong senses of community almost inevitably lead to alternative legal systems. Religious communities throughout history have recognized that they have resources to deal with conflicts that make them mandatory forums for people of the faith. The Jewish community in the Middle Ages, the Mormon community in Utah in the settlement days, Indian communities, and so-called "primitive" communities have always recognized that conflicts are not simply about law, they are about relationships. In such groups, religious and community-based informal "courts" have developed to provide real remedies of restoration and justice when rights are violated and relationships torn.

But Will It Play in Peoria?

All of this might sound like great theology, but not much good for business, contracts, and making one's way in the world. But rather than dismissing 1 Corinthians 6:1 as mere eschatological hope, the lawyers mentioned at the start of this chapter decided to test the validity of the biblical principles. They challenged the church (both in its institutional expression and within the Christian community at large) to develop ways that persons with disputes could consult trained fellow believers for healing and reconciliation. Could 1 Corinthians 6 and Matthew 18 actually help Christian business people resolve partnership disputes, settle contract claims, deal with landlord-tenant problems, intervene in the tragic emotional disputes about child custody, help churches involved in intra-church conflicts and splits, and resolve claims out of wills?

It was with such a set of questions that the Christian Conciliation Service was launched as a special ministry of the Christian Legal Society. This ministry has grown to 30 centers throughout the United States where Christian lawyers, business people, professionals, and pastors have created citywide ministries which encourage Christian persons to use the resources of the Christian community. They work closely with local congregations and other community services to create panels of gifted Christian mediators and arbitrators. These arbitrators help parties assess their claims in the light of biblical teaching and recognize the claims of the Gospel upon their responses.

They then help bring the disputants into a process where there is direct confrontation, clear commitments to justice and righteousness, confession and openness, and an expectation that God can break through the defensiveness and the rights which we so eagerly protect. The results have been astonishing. By no means do all disputants, suddenly in the light of a Bible verse, rush to one another's arms seeking to give away their assets and release their claims. But there have been signs of the presence of Christ and the healing of relationships. The power of the Gospel does break through.

So rapid has been the growth of this commitment in many communities, that a variety of resource materials have been developed to assist churches and local programs to implement these procedures in their own congregations. Training seminars have been developed for mediators and arbitrators. We are challenged to be agents of reconciliation, peacemakers, and healers.

Should Christians Assert Their Legal Rights?

Let's look at four principles that will help Christians determine whether to assert their legal rights.*

1. What are your motives? Why you do something should be considered on an equal plane with what you do. Often your participation in the legal process will depend upon an objective

---

*The following material is based on an outline prepared by University of Missouri (Columbia) law professor Carl Esbeck.

and sincere assessment of your purpose or underlying motive. Impermissible motives include revenge, pride, retribution, retaliation, and self-vindication.

Jesus explains what a Christian's response should be when he is wronged:

> You have heard that it was said, "An eye for an eye, and a tooth for a tooth." But I say to you, do not resist him who is evil; but whoever slaps you on your right cheek, turn to him the other also. And if anyone wants to sue you, and take your shirt, let him have your coat also (Matt. 5:38-40, NASB).

Our relationships must be grounded in love, not in fairness, redress, or retaliation. This passage is not suggesting that we shouldn't oppose evil per se; but we should not oppose the evil person who personally wrongs us. (Compare with Luke 6:27-36.)

Matthew 5:38-48 should not be misinterpreted as an invitation for irresponsibility. These verses do not spell out what our responses should be when:

- the evil person's actions will harm someone else
- our inaction will condone or encourage more misbehavior
- we are faced with widespread social injustice

Jesus made it clear that we should not retaliate against the person who is harming us (v. 39). But our inaction should not be misunderstood as approval of the evil person's deeds. Rather, our response should demonstrate our love for the person, but not for his wrong deed.

> You have heard that it was said, "You shall love your neighbor, and hate your enemy." But I say to you, love your enemies, and pray for those who persecute you. . . . For if you love those who love you, what reward have you? Do not even the tax-gatherers do the same? . . . Do not rejoice when your enemy falls, and do not let your heart be glad when he stumbles (Matt. 5:43-44, 46; Prov. 24:17, NASB).

Paul dealt with this same concept in his letters:

> Never pay back evil for evil to anyone. Respect what is right in the sight of all men. If possible, so far as it depends on you, be at peace with all men. . . . Do not be overcome by evil, but overcome evil with good. . Let all bitterness and wrath and anger and clamor and slander be put away from you, along with malice. And

be kind to one another, tenderhearted, forgiving each other, just
as God in Christ also has forgiven you. . . . Do nothing from selfish-
ness or empty conceit, but with humility of mind let each of you
regard one another as more important than himself; do not merely
look out for your own personal interests, but also for the interests
of others (Rom. 12:17-18, 21; Eph. 4:31-32; Phil. 2:3-4, NASB).

2. *Do your responsibilities or your positions of authority cause
you to assert legal rights on behalf of people you may be accountable to?* In some cases, you may be expected to go to bat for
someone who has entrusted you with certain duties—your church,
your employer, your local government.

Specific scriptural examples of positions that would require
this include:

- Judges   (Deut. 19:17-21)
- Apostles   (Eph. 4:11-15)
- Overseers   (1 Tim. 3:1-7)
- Deacons   (1 Tim. 3:8-13)
- Elders   (1 Tim. 5:17-20)

3. *On what law are you relying?* Do you want to assert your
legal rights because you feel justified by Scripture, by culture, or
by legislation? A comparison of God's character with man's laws
should help you decide.

God is the embodiment of truth and justice; His works demonstrate these characteristics (Ps. 111:7). His precepts are right; by
them, His servant is warned (19:7-11). In Psalm 119 the psalmist
repeatedly praises God for His law and asks Him for a better
understanding of it:

Teach me, O Lord, the way of Thy statutes, and I shall observe
it to the end. Give me understanding, that I may observe Thy law,
and keep it with all my heart (119:33-34, NASB). (Also see vv.
35-40, 97-104, and 129-136.)

Man's laws can be divided into two categories, *malum in se* and
malum prohibitum. *Malum in se* refers to an act that is wrong in
itself. Because of its very nature, it conflicts with the principles
of natural, moral, and public law. *Malum prohibitum* refers to a
thing which is wrong because it is prohibited, but is not inherently
immoral.

4. What responsibilities to others are involved? When you are the defendant in a legal case or when you are being sued, you should consider your obligations to your family and as steward over the property God has entrusted to you (1 Tim. 5:8).

Cases involving the government are usually either civil or criminal in nature. We are told to obey the government (Rom. 13:1-7; 1 Peter 2:13-17); yet there are examples in Scripture of believers who refused to obey the law when it conflicted with God's higher law (see Dan. 6:1-24; Acts 4:18-20).

As for matters of a criminal nature, we should work within the legal system to obtain our freedom (see Acts 22:22—26:32). If we are guilty of something we are accused of, we should confess our wrongdoing (1 John 1:9). But we are still responsible for our actions even when the system is unjust. We, not the system, will have to answer to God for our reactions to the legal rulings made for or against us in criminal matters.

* * * * *

Use the principles you've studied in this chapter to decide how you would handle the following cases:

Danny Goodfellow, a Christian, is 31 years old, married, and the father of three young daughters. Danny has always been an excellent athlete and an avid water and snow skier. He is a college graduate and has a successful business and promising career in real estate development.

Almost three years ago Danny had surgery at Presbyterian Hospital Center for fusion of a portion of his back. Though the hospital is owned by an institutional church, it is largely secularized in its operation and most of the staff are not Christians. The operation was successful, but during post-operative therapy an employee of the hospital lifted Danny improperly, resulting in a fracture of his backbone. The corrective surgery was performed by Dr. Andersen, who has had privileges at the hospital for five years.

After the corrective surgery, Danny had constant and severe back pain and has had 11 more operations. It is the opinion of Danny's current doctors and other experts that Dr. Andersen did not follow proper medical procedures in the corrective surgery and is liable for malpractice. The only means left surgically to alleviate Danny's pain is to sever his spinal cord, which would leave Danny a paraplegic.

One year ago Danny went to a lawyer specializing in medical malpractice and brought suit against the hospital. He did not name Dr. Andersen in the suit. But the hospital and its insurance carrier believe that the primary fault lies with Dr. Andersen. The hospital is unwilling to offer any more than $10,000 in settlement and would rather go to trial than pay more money.

Danny's lawyer has told him that unless he names Dr. Andersen as a defendant, his chances of receiving an adequate award at trial are substantially diminished. Danny, both personally and through his pastor, has attempted to speak to Dr. Andersen about the matter. But Dr. Andersen, possibly on the advice of his insurance carrier, has refused to meet with Danny.

Danny is now in constant pain and is often unable to sleep at night. He is only able to work two days a week and has been told by his doctors that he will probably have to stop working completely in two years. Danny has used up his medical insurance coverage and estimates that his medical bills will be at least $5,000 a year for the rest of his life. Danny does not want to "cash in" on his misery, but merely cover his substantial medical expenses and avoid the welfare roles. Danny's wife is not working because she feels her proper role as a mother dictates that she stay home with the young children.

Within two weeks Danny must decide whether to sue Dr. Andersen, or else he will be forever barred by the statute of limitations from bringing the action. Danny wants to do the right thing and now seeks your advice.

* * * * *

Ruth is a Christian and a third-year medical student. She claims she has just been expelled from the local state university medical school because she refused to perform abortions contrary to direct orders of her superiors. An attorney has advised her that she has a good claim against the university for violating her First Amendment freedom of religion. She can sue for $50,000 or an injunction to get back into school, or both. She comes to you for advice. What would you tell her?

12

A Worldly Faith

Answer the following statements true or false:

1. Christians must become more politically organized   T   F
to protect our values.

2. The principle of separation of church and state   T   F
requires that religious ideas and institutions ought to stay
out of politics.

3. Christian principle largely supports conservative   T   F
political goals and a coalition around such objectives is
essential.

* * * * *

It should be observed that, if a systematic religion is true at all,
intrusion on its part into politics is not only legitimate, but is the
very work it comes into the world to do. Being by hypothesis,
enlightened supernaturally, it is able to survey the conditions and
consequences of any kind of action much better than the wisest
legislator . . . so that the spheres of systematic religion and politics—far from being independent—are in principle identical.

          —George Santayana

Since the end of the 1970s, the emergence of evangelical Christians into politics has attracted both widespread attention and
criticism. The 1980s have seen vigorous political and legal action
by conservative groups. Religious groups took credit for playing
a major role in the 1980 defeats of six U.S. Senators: George

McGovern, Frank Church, John Culver, Birch Bayh, and Gaylord Nelson. Jerry Falwell declared: "The moralists in America have had enough. We are joining hands together for the changing, the rejuvenation of a nation." Speaking at a rally for God and Country on the steps of the New Jersey capitol a week after the election, Falwell said: "We registered 4 million in the churches last year to vote that had never voted before. We activated another 10 million. . . . We have just begun to fight." The American Civil Liberties Union declared in a fund-raising letter: "If the Moral Majority has its way, you'd better start praying."

Liberal churchmen have long taken active and aggressive political postures on social issues. More mainstream evangelists such as Carl Henry have long pleaded for evangelical involvement. But most evangelicals were reluctant to come out of their suburban churches and do political and legal warfare. Now, however, those who eschewed engagement with public affairs have left their comfortable pews for campaigning in the streets, mailboxes, and halls of legislators.

What is it that has driven Christian people from their prayer meetings to the messy world of politics? Surely a major factor has been the moral crisis of our society. "The West is ineluctably slipping toward the abyss. Western societies are losing more and more of their religious essence as they thoughtlessly yield up their younger generation to atheism," warns Alexander Solzhenitsyn. The moral character of American society has by some measures been in decline for decades. But the last straw has come with the emergence of the drug culture, the sexual revolution, the advocacy of gay rights, and the threats to family life. Abortion, suicide, and divorce are rampant. Something has to be done. Only a spiritual awakening can save our nation.

But some people have not welcomed the new political involvement of Christian groups. They complain of mixing religion and politics. In 1980 the American Civil Liberties Union accused the Moral Majority of being engaged in an attempt to "capture the power of government and use it to establish a nightmare of religious and political orthodoxy." With less than candor, they accused the group of being involved in an effort "not to preserve traditional American values, but to overthrow them." That criticism came from a group that has engaged for decades in defending those who would overturn our society's prevailing moral values.

Let us dispense quickly with a few of the common, but inadequate, criticisms of the evangelical movement's involvement in politics. First, some people contend that Christians are thrusting private and personal moral issues into politics where such issues do not belong. But evangelicals have not raised these moral issues to the level of public debate. Evangelicals have not suddenly changed their views about the law and the relationship of moral principles to public law. While debate about what morality is appropriate for public law is legitimate, the notion that morality has no place in law is absurd.

Second, some people believe that promoting moral values which have religious sanctions and origins somehow interferes with the separation between church and state. Surely the church cannot be silenced in its moral teaching because an issue is now of public interest and political debate. Does the church lose some right of discourse when issues are urgent, but retain those rights when they are dormant? Can the government preclude the church's participation in moral conversation merely by moving politically into the zone? That argument would allow the state to define the realm of legitimate church/religious discussion to those areas it had not yet annexed. For the church to speak about sexuality, abortion, or pornography is not to suddenly step across a boundary into the realm of politics. It is frightening to see attempts to use the tax power to silence the church's moral teachings.

Third, the evangelicals involved in politics are not demagogues seeking to destroy the character of American liberty by creating a totalitarian state along their personal moral grounds. To be sure, under the vision of society as seen by these persons, the pornographer would be restrained, the abortionist would not be funded with tax monies, and there would be a return to state support for a traditional moral code. After all, strong minorities on the Court, probably majorities in many state legislatures and the U.S. Congress, and certainly the historic pattern in our nation saw such moral support from law as not at all contrary to liberty.

To suddenly picture advocates of U.S. legal policy up to recent years as being barbarians is either deliberately dishonest or woefully ignorant.

What Is Needed?

The thrust of evangelicals into politics must be based on much more than frustration with contemporary morals. Central to any Christian involvement must be a biblically based perspective.

In approaching the world, Christians have given almost exclusive attention to Scripture passages which describe us as "strangers and pilgrims." We have been taught, "Love not the world, neither the things that are in the world. If any man love the world, the love of the Father is not in him" (1 John 2:15). A government, clearly "worldly," was seen then as evil, as a captive of the principalities and powers, or at least as being so "this worldly" that it did not warrant the expenditure of the church's and believers' limited resources.

But the "world" which is to be avoided and resisted is not the world of society, government, and culture. Christians are rediscovering that history is the arena of God's revelation. God reveals Himself not in the context of "other worldly" experiences or mystical religion, but in the *events* of this world—the Creation, the Exodus, the Incarnation, the Resurrection. Christianity is, in this sense, an extremely "worldly" religion. Biblical Christians get excited, not so much in the face of an ecstatic experience, but when they see "justice roll down like waters and righteousness as an everflowing stream" (Amos 5:24, NASB).

Similarly, by accepting the lordship of Christ we insist that every arena of human life be subject to Christ's authority. Therefore, as His ambassadors and as witnesses to His reign, the Gospel must be declared in sanitary districts and school systems as much as in churches. There can be no escape to "religion," no mere willingness to carve out a zone of activity exempt from government authority in which Christians may privately huddle till the end. Rather, we are commissioned to declare God as the Creator of all, the Judge of all nations, and ultimately the builder not only of a new heaven, but a new earth. Our task, therefore, cannot be merely to "get along" in the world, or merely see it as an occasion for some good works or as an arena in which to find souls who may be saved. It is a place of discipleship, a place to declare God's truth, to work for justice, to speak for righteousness.

With this theological commitment, evangelicals are empowered to tackle public issues that shape our society. No longer can we be content with passivity about our public lives. With this in mind, let's identify some basic principles that should guide Christian involvement in law and politics.

Developing a Biblical Style

Our commitment to Jesus Christ will control the legitimate *means* we use in our public involvement. While at times the exercise of political muscle and power may be appropriate to achieve justice, Christians will be hesitant to see Christian political engagement as merely another interest group or caucus.

Evangelicals are not used much to direct political power. Those who drink the wine of power are often not only intoxicated by it, but are captured by its illusions. The tendency to engage in power politics is strong today. But without a biblical and philosophic commitment, that power may turn upon the evangelical. Power itself is by no means evil, but it is indeed dangerous when exercised outside the context of communities, without accountability, without humanity. But when does the use of political power obviate the very spiritual values sought? What are the certifiers, of power—mere majorities, or tradition, or "right"? What goals may be achieved by power and what may not?

A prophetic perspective suggests a strategy of a "servant" role, a style which sees the faith community as existing not simply for its own self but to serve the nation, even the world; that through the faith community, the whole world will know the love, justice, and glory of God. And it will do this "not by might, nor by power, but by My Spirit" (Zech. 4:6).

The prophetic tradition does indeed call for the moral and prophetic witness to the nation—but it does so from a curious posture. It is a posture of political weakness and servanthood.

Like Israel itself, the prophet is weak and helpless before Baby-
lon, Assyrian, and Egyptian might; and she dare not trust in
chariots and swords, but rather upon the powerful Word of the
Lord. The prophet, though morally earnest and weeping over the
tragedy, is essentially a politically powerless person. Christians
should have few illusions about their likely political success, noting that prophets were largely honored posthumously. Faithfulness is more important than success.

Distinguishing God's Agenda

Christians must resist the temptation to claim that a particular
political persuasion expresses God's will. The tragedy of too
much Christian involvement in politics is that its positions have
reflected a high degree of "worldliness." That is, the positions
seem to have emerged more from political pre-dispositions of
individuals than from a fundamental biblical posture.

The agenda of Christians often seems both too narrow and too
broad. It is far too narrow in its failure to be international in scope
and in its focus exclusively on personal moral ethics rather than
giving equal attention to fundamental issues of justice and ethics
in our society such as racism, business ethics, poverty, the arms
race, and economic issues. It is not that there is a particular
perspective that such persons must have on these issues, but to
fail to recognize the profound systemic issues of righteousness in
our world is to forfeit the right to speak with moral authority. If
evangelicals wish to speak for liberty and freedom, we must claim
the full-orbed powerful biblical commitment to justice which again
marks the prophetic commitments—a justice which cries out for
the widow and the orphan, the poor and the oppressed, as well
as for the rights of the Christian school and the prayer group at
the campus.

If part of the problem is that the agenda has been too narrow,
it has also in some sense been far too broad, reflecting the inabili-
ty to distinguish fundamental moral issues from political questions
which rest in a different dimension. In some sense there seems
to be "worldliness," from a biblical perspective, in the agenda of
some religious groups. Their agendas seem too often to reflect the

cultural and political philosophy of their socio-cultural environs and the guidance of pollsters rather than any profoundly biblical agenda. Born-again politics looks far too often just like the "old folks" politics. When an agenda includes everything from opposition to abortion to resistance to the graduated income tax, from concerns for family life to membership in the United Nations, there is indeed confusion if not an unholy alliance. We should recognize that there is a substantial difference in the level of moral discourse between such issues as abortion and the Panama Canal Treaty.

We must also recognize that all of our political judgments, our predispositions to a particular political philosophy, whether traditionally labeled "conservative" or "liberal," are subject to the discipline of God's Word. It may well be that biblical faithfulness will include certain positions frequently endorsed by conservative groups, and other positions endorsed by liberal groups. The label the world gives the viewpoint is irrelevant. What is central is the teaching of Scripture.

Unless we can distinguish genuine moral issues from those issues which are much less clear and subject to political dialogue, we will not only lose the potential for a strong collective witness on great issues, but we will dissipate our energies. This requires the recognition that on many issues there will be significant differences of opinion within the Christian community. What some will question or oppose, others will affirm.

All Things Shall Pass Away
Christians must resist the tendency to an exaggerated nationalism. America has no special claim on divinity. All nations and all governments are subject to God's judgment. We may be enthusiastically patriotic, acknowledging the tremendous heritage of liberty and faith which is ours. We may rightly argue that American political philosophy and practice represent one of the highest examples of political life in the world. But we must not confuse God's order with the American order. We cannot be for God and country—if those two are meant to be on equal footing.

We dare not "civilize" Christian faith in terms of American

economic and political life so that it loses its capacity to criticize the spirit of this age. "Civil religion eases tensions where biblical religion creates them," observes Schlossberg. Capitalism, democracy, constitutional law—all of these great aspects of political life may become idols of modern man.

The Limits of Worldly Justice

As urgent and biblically required as involvement with the world is, a Christian can have no illusion about what the state may achieve. French theologian and lawyer Jacques Ellul noted:

> The Christian will plunge in to the world in order to have an influence on the world, not in the hope of making it a paradise, but simply in order to make it tolerable—not in order to diminish the opposition between this world and the kingdom of God, but simply in order to modify the opposition between the disorder of this world and the order of preservation that God wills for it—not in order to bring the kingdom of God, but in order that the Gospel will be proclaimed, that all men may hear the Good News.

We must recognize the limits of the political process. Ellul was perhaps too narrow, but government and law are not intended to encompass all spiritual or even temporal good. Government has a more limited sphere. We can eagerly work for an effective government while simultaneously knowing that even great government is, and ought to be, limited. We must work elsewhere for other important aspects of our growth and values. If we only strengthen the government and neglect other institutions such as the family, the church, and private associations, we have invited tyranny. We must not use government to exercise power in our behalf when that represents an illegitimate role for government.

Too often the Christian's public stance has been exclusively negative. It is not enough to merely identify those government policies we may find inadequate or offensive. While opposing something is quite legitimate, we must also offer positive contributions. In education, for example, we must do more than criticize textbooks or humanistic values. What can we contribute by way of curriculum designs and support for teachers to improve all aspects of education? If we fail to participate in the long-term process of making our institutions effective, our complaints will not likely be heard.

Christians might well reassess the tendency to see the national level as the place of most effective public service and political involvement. The Supreme Court, Congress, and the Executive Branch are frequent targets of political action. And surely much of our national life emanates from those sources. Yet in many instances, the *real* shape of a culture—its values, attitudes, and policies—are formed in much more local expressions: school boards, city councils, state governments. If we seek to participate in political life, we should begin at the local level.

Conclusion

Evangelicals rightly insist that religion, and specifically the Christian faith and Judeo-Christian ethics, has a significant message for the character of the national ethos. Indeed, it would be hard to contend that social values and moral norms have not historically emerged from and been sustained by deep religious commitments. Where, if not from religion, directly or indirectly, shall society muster the content and commitment to focus upon urgent world issues of hunger, bioethics, nuclear armaments, and human rights?

Evangelicals are absolutely correct in insisting on the right of persons to engage in political activity out of their religious commitments. Why should those commitments be excluded? The alternative would be tragic. Shall we leave to mere technicians the tasks of shaping justice and freedom? Rubrics such as "separation of church and state" and "wall of separation" are no longer very helpful in assessing the role of religion in a fundamentally pluralist society.

Christians are right in pressing society to face a most difficult issue—namely, the limits on individual freedom necessary for the conditions of freedom and the existence of society. Is a lover of liberty compelled to allow the pornographer equal liberty with the philosopher? We have certainly decided that some conduct—racism, fraud, discrimination—is morally incompatible with our national commitment. The issue of the scope of the enforcement of morality by the state is complex, but not at all irrelevant.

Evangelicals are right and perform a critical public service when they demand that society recognize the right of religious freedom and that those rights adhere not only to persons, but to institutions and ministries. Government, however benevolent, is only one locus of power in a society, and society is enriched when it maximizes religious freedom. They are correct who note the hostility to spiritual values evident in many governmental policies, and in their rejection of the pretensions of the state's encompassing authority.

The evangelical discovery of law and politics is a biblically sound, politically legitimate, and socially urgent recognition of cultural responsibility. Evangelicals have both a public right and duty to help shape our society's character.